W9-ATH-160

Ordinary
Paradise

Also by Laura Furman

The Glass House

The Shadow Line

Watch Time Fly

Tuxedo Park

Bookworms: Great Writers and Readers Celebrate Reading
(with Elinore Standard)

.

Ordinary Paradise

Laura Furman

Winedale Publishing

Houston

PUBLISHED BY WINEDALE PUBLISHING CO.

Copyright © 1998 by Laura Furman
All rights reserved under International and Pan-American
Copyright Conventions.
Published in the United States by Winedale Publishing Co., Houston
Distributed by the Texas A&M University Press Consortium

A portion of this book appeared, in slightly different form, in *Mirabella*.
Grateful acknowledgment is made to the Society of Authors as Literary
Representative of the Estate of Katherine Mansfield for permission to quote from
The Letters and Journals of Katherine Mansfield, C.K. Stead, ed.
(London: Allen Lane, 1977)

Portrait of "Minnie, 1939" by Sylvan Furman, courtesy of the author
Photograph on page 105, by Charles Stein, and on page 157, by Carol Cohen
Burton, courtesy of the author
Other photographs from the author's collection

Library of Congress Cataloging-in-Publication Data
Furman, Laura
Ordinary Paradise / by Laura Furman
p. cm.
ISBN 0—965—7468—4—4
1. Grief. 2. Loss (Psychology)
3. Mothers—Death—Psychological Aspects.
4. Mothers and daughters. 5. Furman, Laura—Family. I. Title.
BF575.G7F87 1998
813'.54—dc21 [B] 98-27467 CIP

Manufactured in the United States of America
2 4 6 8 9 7 5 3
First Edition

Book design by Harriet Correll

For Miriam M. Kaye

Is it not possible that the rage for confession, autobiography, especially for memories of earliest childhood, is explained by our persistent yet mysterious belief in a self which is continuous and permanent; which, untouched by all we acquire and all we shed, pushes a green spear through the dead leaves and through the mould, thrusts a scaled bud through years of darkness until, one day, the light discovers it and shakes the flowers free and—we are alive—we are flowering for our moment upon the earth? This is the moment which, after all, we live for—the moment of direct feeling when we are most ourselves and least personal.

Katherine Mansfield

Acknowledgments

My love and gratitude go to Joel Warren Barna and Solomon Barna.

I give my thanks for their invaluable encouragement to Glenn and Kathleen Cambor, John Davidson, Lynn Freed, Elinore Standard, and Aryeh Lev Stollman. I am grateful to my colleagues Elizabeth Warnock Fernea and Millicent Marcus for their support. Thanks, as well, to the University of Texas at Austin for a U.R.I. grant.

Preface

I began this book after years of writing fiction, using my writing time not to imagine but to remember. Only when I was well involved did I question what I was doing, for memory seemed like a suspect state to court, an avoidance of the present—in fact, the opposite of living in the present.

Two principals of my story are dead, a third is aged. My sisters and I live thousands of miles apart. The apartments where we were a family are out of our possession or changed forever, and the country house where I was happiest is occupied by the third set of people since our decamping thirty years ago. Best of all, I am a wife and a mother. I have a family of my own. Why spend so long dwelling on the past, so long as it takes to remember, to contemplate, and to write? We live in a time when getting over grief and loss is the applauded course, almost a ritual of maturity, and I have let go, as others have, of grievances, habits, affections. Yet there is an experience which I cannot consign to another self or another time, and that is my mother's death.

It is a touchstone memory that I've circled and abandoned, thinking I've understood all that happened, and yet I've returned to contemplate the memory time and again.

I started to write this book in 1988, when things started to shift in my experience of fiction-writing. Metaphor had carried me from my adolescence through my thirties, and it was beginning to interest me less. In 1986 I had published a novel that had to do with keeping secrets from children, and when the publisher asked me to prepare a speech about the novel for a tour, I wrote about the Sleeping Beauty, and about the consequences of maintaining a sleeping stance, unconsciously willing self-ignorance. My heroine had stayed asleep and only a drastic action by her daughter forced her into awakening. The experience of composing the speech and delivering it eight or ten times made me begin to wonder who the speech was about—my heroine or me. I was about to be forty. I'd been sleeping, now I was waking up, finding blackness and secrets. I needed to understand my own story so badly that I stopped being interested in writing imaginary stories, and needed to construct my own. I found that I couldn't remember my story well enough to tell it to myself.

When I was a child, I wanted to remember every passing moment of my life. I stopped sometimes and told myself, *You'll remember this always,* but what I have remembered is the commemorating. For years I couldn't, or thought I couldn't, remember my childhood. I couldn't, as others could, recite my family's history or even tell their characters and their habits. Often I felt indifferent to the past: Yes, these things happened and now they are over. It was a godlike point of view that left me feeling displaced. My remembered story gives me a home.

And then there is the question of accuracy. Many memoirs

(especially by fiction writers) begin by declaring that the text that follows is true. I fully intend to be truthful because otherwise there is no point in writing this, but I can't believe that what follows will be the truth. Family life without a tragic disruption is complicated enough, and for a family member to claim the flag of truth is hubristic. The promise I make that's within my power to fulfill is to be honest. I saw a black and white photograph in a dream, and the photograph was torn at the top corners from folding and from age. The five of us were in it: my parents, my two sisters, and I. We are sitting on the ground, all jumbled together, Daddy kneeling behind Mommy and sticking his head forward so that they are cheek to cheek. There is no such photograph of us together, nor souvenir, except those of us who remain. My memories are no one else's. I can only describe what I see in my photograph. I ordered my story in a chronology of feeling rather than a strict sequence of events, because that is the way memory works.

I dream of the places we lived together: 55 West Ninety-fifth Street and 164 State Street and Schooley's Mountain and West End Avenue. I dream of my mother's return, and my stepmother appears in different guises, often that of a friend. My father, now dead also, appears—no longer thin and bent by illness but a robust man, free from pain, including the pain of being my father, and the pleasure. In my dreams he is what he never was in life, free from attachment, though I suspect he yearned for such freedom and shrank from it too.

I wrote so that I might connect with the parents in my dreams and connect also with the child and her sisters, the childhood friends and their parents, then in their beautiful prime. I wrote to see my family story as an adult, not as a child, and also to recapture the child's view. I wrote because I missed the dead, my mother whom I never knew when I was grown up and my father, of whom I thought daily, understanding a little something more, putting together a piece of the puzzle, or simply remembering.

The reader may ask, as I do, Why didn't I ask my father enough questions while he was alive to satisfy my curiosity and feed my hunger for adult knowledge about my mother's life and death? I did, and he evaded answering. He didn't like confrontation or self-examination, though he was thoughtful, even preoccupied much of the time. He had a kind of deference to life, a way of stepping aside, hoping perhaps to let inevitable troubles move past. My father didn't believe in remembering or at least in handed-down memory. ("Oral history," he called it, refusing to write down the name of the town in Ukraine where his father was born.) In the mid-fifties, he wrote to his father who had asked him to act for him in a family dispute, "I feel strongly that old sores should not be re-opened, and that if there were problems in the past, there is very little point in letting them affect our own lives at this time." One of life's large problems—the death of my mother—left my father with a certain amount of energy for survival and little left over for sharing memories. He died on June 9, 1992, the fifty-second anniversary of his marriage to my mother, and I choose to believe that part of him was remembering all along, as I have.

Nothing out of the ordinary happened. My father did not molest me. My stepmother did not send me into the woods with a hired killer. Nothing sensational happened to demand the reader's attention to my story except that, as in families where physical harm has been done, a cover story was invented, elaborated on, rewritten, codified, and maintained. The reality of my experience of the world was denied in my family. My origin, my basis for self-knowledge and therefore for growth and maturing, was deemed unmentionable.

I have always been timid about my family's past and my own, as if the past were a party I wasn't invited to. When I spent time remembering, I did so guiltily, not wishing to be caught wondering about the past. The past dominated my life and informed my present, though I didn't see that except in fleeting glimpses of understanding.

So for me undertaking a memoir was a difficult task for which I might not be suited by nature, but to which I felt drawn. I wanted for however long it took to pin up the pictures, read through the papers and letters, to try to figure out, in simple terms, what happened: how my family was formed and how it dissolved and how the second family, willy nilly, took its place. Survival sounds too dramatic for what took place, but my survival seemed in question to me when I was young. My life now is an ordinary paradise I thought I would never live to enjoy.

A report to the reader: If I've learned one thing from writing this memoir, it is that denial is a vast ocean, not the discreet hillock I'd always thought it to be. *She's in denial. She's in denial about her mother's death.* Said quickly and glibly, the word darts over the living meaning. It has taken me decades to feel the events in my story, and the feeling still has power over me. "In denial" is a storm that gathers force and picks up objects as it goes, making it more dangerous than before. "Denial" is a constant habit, part of my skin and my brain; it is what happens before understanding or thinking; it is the cloud I carry around me. Depression is secondary to denial, though it carries more weight as a word. There is no enzyme stimulant to be used against denial. It was there all along in our family. The way my parents chose to deal with my mother's illness and death made the seeds spread onto my fertile ground.

To some extent, we all grow up alone in our families and all siblings grow up in different families. Parents and step-parents raise children in orbs the children wouldn't recognize. My family is no exception. I don't speak for my sisters or my father or my mother. Out of respect for the privacy of my living relatives and friends, I've changed many names. I speak only for myself and I do it as selfishly as I'm able. Writing is the best way I know to remember us all.

Laura Furman
Austin, Texas

Minnie Airov Furman, age thirty-four

One summer night, at high altitude in Colorado, I dreamed that my mother hadn't died—not on May 14, 1959, nor any other time. All this time, she had been in Paris, living under the name of Aida Major and pursuing her career as a singer.

A postcard from Aida Major, a black and white postcard, lay on the table where the mail always waited in the apartment on West End Avenue. It was our old dining room table, its leaves folded now and never opened for family occasions. It stood, modern and bare, across from the little pine chest that still held our ice skates, flanked by my stepmother's grander, darker furniture: a desk that opened out and I never opened it; the Chinese cabinet painted with a scene of peasants carrying water up a cruel vertical mountain. In the image of her on the postcard, my mother looked just like herself though her almost Oriental eyes were deeper sunk than I had known them—an effect enhanced by kohl?—and her curly black hair formed a crown around her head. She'd been leading a rough life, anyone could see that. She faced the camera with complete candor as if she no longer had a thing to hide and nothing to pretend. She looked weary on the postcard but more of a personality than I had known my mother to be. Of course, I had known her only as a private person, Minnie Airov Furman, not as Aida Major, opera singer of Paris. The message on the postcard was that she'd be coming back to New York soon because she was ill and needed help.

I stood in the foyer. There was a hum in the apartment, preparations for a special meal, women talking and laughing, and all the women were related to me—sisters, stepmother, stepsister. They glanced at me as they passed, carrying tablecloths and silver, plates and crystal. They hesitated to speak to me. I felt as I had so often in my family, that they feared me and feared for me.

They had known all along what I had just discovered, and they considered it neither miraculous nor noteworthy that Aida Major was ill and penniless and needing help. To them, it was the inevitable consequence of her choice of life.

I woke from my dream of Aida Major, assaulted by the idea that my mother was alive. This hopeless possibility followed me through the day of hiking in the mountains until it was replaced by another thought: that, decades later, the medium through which I felt most intensely was still my mother's death.

～

When the cancer that killed her permitted her to do little else, my mother continued to move our car from one side of the street to the other according to New York City parking regulations, keeping faithful to the routine of her frugal, complicated life. This memory infuriates me. It is proof of a certain kind of incompetence and paralysis that feels like a family legacy: to be unable to lift a finger to make things easier. But really it's about money. It's about being unable to use money to make things easier. It's true that parking on the street was free and we did not have extra money to spend on a garage, but if her illness was not an emergency requiring extraordinary spending, what was? I hate to think of her moving the car on alternate mornings. I hate it that I can still get caught in the labyrinth of wondering what else to do, absent the possibility of spending money on a garage to spare her. She might have objected to a garage—if she'd given in to that luxury it would have been a recognition of how little time she had left. So off she went to park the car. Otherwise, she stayed in bed, she who didn't take naps or rest, she who was busy and moving always, keeping things smooth, clean, and orderly.

One day while my mother lay in her bedroom, I took a friend into the bathroom with me and we shared a cigarette. I had started to experiment with smoking, but I wasn't yet buying them on my own. Probably my friend stole the cigarette from her mother or I from my sister or father. We must have been smoking and giggling a long time, and there was my mother, sick, on the other side of the plaster wall. Did I think she was deaf and had lost her sense of smell? Or that she was dead already? She might have asked this as she rose from her bed and pounded on the door, calling, "What are you doing in there?" We giggled, scared, and tried to fan the smoke out the narrow window. I called out, "In a minute," to shoo my mother away. We opened the door. My mother stood in the hall, the robe barely covering her swollen, scarred body. I helped her back to bed. My friend went home. We had smoked and giggled obliviously, and then there was my mother's voice, and I realized that I had done what I never wanted to do—I'd hurt my mother and incurred her wrath. I'd forced her to lift her damaged body. I'd made her raise her voice to me.

Had she lived, we'd have had more scenes. Five people in a small apartment, there would have been more spreading wings and testing boundaries as people say so casually, as if each border raid doesn't have its victims. But she died and so it seemed that I was not just careless or silly but that I was evil.

∽

I dream, and have for years, that she is alive and that nothing ever changed. I'm happy and complete while dreaming: I am walking down Ninety-fifth Street on the long stretch between the canopy of Sixty-five and the entrance to our Fifty-five, and I look ahead and there is my mother. She is standing with her shopping cart and she sees me before I see her. Even seeing her I don't realize for a minute that she is there, but she sees me, and she looks at me fondly and steadily, waiting for me to understand. I move toward her and there the dream ends.

I don't live in New York, and I haven't for twenty-six years. I don't walk down that street.

∽

What is my mother wearing? She's twenty-six and it is 1938. She is at the beach with my father and some friends. The beach is Provincetown, Massachusetts. My mother is sturdy, black-haired, and easy in her body. Her bathing-suit is skirted, the bodice flowered and strapless, a wide band of solid color at the top. She doesn't swim much but likes the feel of the sun as she lies on the windy beach, hearing at the distance her friends calling to each other, my father's voice, the seagulls. On the boardwalk and out to sea in the afternoon in an excursion boat, she's in striped Capri pants and the long sleeves of her bateau-neck pullover are pushed up to her elbows. As for the town itself, it looks provisional, as if Provincetown in 1938 might not last. A woman in a straw hat is seated by the side of a board-and-batten wall, painting at her easel.

Before my mother marries, when she's still a working girl, she has a splendid winter coat with a lamb collar, the kinky fur draping obediently over her shoulders, making the coat warmer than it has a right to be in the New York damp.

Later, when she is my mother, she doesn't dress like the other Upper West Side mothers in spike heels and straight tight skirts. Her shoes are low-heeled and a little clunky. She has a red tweed suit for dress-up and for formidable occasions, such as going to school to find out what the second-grade teacher is doing to me. The same tweed suit, accented with black buttons, is hanging in her closet when she dies six years later. She has blue jeans for the country, some of them pedal-pusher length, full-cut and comfortable over her stomach and hips. When she's painting the white trim of the brown-shingled house or weeding the vegetable garden, she wears a stretched-out bathing suit with floppy wide-cut short shorts over it, or a discarded shirt of my father's. She should cover her hair and protect her skin, but she doesn't, any more than she breaks the habit of biting inside her cheek. For country dress-up she wears Capri pants just like the ones she had in Provincetown (maybe the same ones) or sundresses with full skirts. She likes tee-shirts with horizontal stripes, or white ones with dark ribbing at the collar and sleeves.

At the end of the day when she's driving to her friend Faith's for dinner, she dons tortoise-shell sunglasses that are flattering with a tailored white shirt and a sweater draped over her shoulders. She wears a light gray skirt to complete the ensemble. Her girls are with her. Two have run off with Faith's daughters; her youngest stays beside her, jiggling the arm of the chaise longue. It's summer, high summer, and they've come a little early for the evening. Before she joins Faith, before the husbands join them and pour drinks, before the feeding of the children, she stays a moment on the patio. There's a white clapboard wall behind her that's absorbed the heat of the day and it feels good. She puts her feet up for a moment of inaction. She's wondering that she started one place and got to another, that as she went she's gathered daughters, husband, house. She has only one window left to putty and paint and then she's done with the second story. Everything might be different and was.

 ⁓

My father painted an oil portrait of my mother in 1939 when she was twenty-seven, around the time of their marriage. The dominant colors of the portrait are mustard yellow, faded apple green, and pale maroon, crimson on her lips. The painting is much influenced by Matisse, especially in the simplification of forms—the patterning of the drapes behind her; the green upholstery of the armchair she sits in; the simple, outlined drawing of her yellow blouse. She looks like one of Matisse's Odalisques but she is distinctly my mother. She looks careful in the portrait, holding herself very still for the painter, and looking off to the side, not straight at him. I can hear him ordering her to stay that way, warning her not to move. The first time she left me with a baby sitter, I went to the painting, looking for her. I thought if I cried enough she would reappear. Now the painting hangs in the room where I write and has since my father gave it to me in 1987. I wondered at the time why he was giving it to me, if perhaps he himself was seriously ill, but I took it, glad to have something of her.

The prime of my mother's life was short and more complicated than I could have seen then because her prime was my happy childhood. My father and sisters did not enter into my satisfaction. They were my family, but my mother was the background of my consciousness.

Decades after her death I wrote to a woman who was my father's lifelong friend and asked her to tell me what my mother was like. The friend answered that my mother was the most serene person she had ever known, calm and contented, happy in her life as wife and mother and housewife, and this at a time when other women were chafing at their roles. My mother was not college-educated and hadn't grown up with any money at all: Did the friend patronize her, judge her simple not to resent woman's ancient roles? I read the letter again and realized that it only confirmed my luck, that I was raised in the company of a mother who wanted to be with me.

My mother, Minnie Airov Furman, came to New York City from Atlanta, Georgia. She was born in Barnsboro, Pennsylvania, a coal mining town near Pittsburgh, and her father Morris owned a junk business. My grandfather was a widower with one son, Sam, when he married my grandmother, Ida, and they had four children—Sophie, Minnie, Molly, and Joseph. Morris's disintegration from Huntington's Chorea and the family's poverty defined my mother's childhood. He was misdiagnosed, thought to be mad, and was in and out of mental hospitals, a volatile figure. The family moved south. There were relatives in Chattanooga, and the Airovs settled in Atlanta. My mother had rheumatic fever when she graduated from secretarial school and stayed another year at home. She left Atlanta for New York, returning once for her mother's funeral and again fifteen years later for a niece's wedding.

My mother spent twenty-five years in New York, nineteen of them married to my father. When they met she was working as a secretary to the director of Lavanburg Corner House, a home for Jewish boys on the Lower East Side. She was living there when she met my father, and so was he, as a young social worker. Since it was the Depression, room and board along with the small salary made their jobs even more desirable. It was summer. Daddy's college girlfriend was away, and by the time she returned, my parents were in love or engaged or committed to one another. The college girlfriend became the mother of a beautiful girl I went to camp with, and it might have been possible when I learned this to feel the net of relationship protecting me. As it was, my mother was dead by then, and I felt that my campmate's mother had been cheated or tricked by my mother and that it was my fault.

I have a Western Union telegram with a blue band across the top and a yellow scroll on which "Congratulations" is printed in type often used by synagogues, sent June 9, 1940, the day my parents were married: "Best wishes for a long life prosperity health and happiness," and it is signed by her father and brothers, "Papa Joe and Sam."

∽

On July 1, 1946, my parents bought a house on Schooley's Mountain, in a dairy-farming area near Long Valley, Morris County, New Jersey. My sister Valerie was three years old and I, eight months. For another couple, two small children might have been a reason not to buy a summer and weekend place that needed years of work and money when there was none, but my parents required the house and the work it demanded, the projects and plans that reached far into the future. I calculate this in retrospect, extrapolating love from fact.

Every surface in the brown-shingled, red-roofed, white-trimmed house was touched by their hands. In the kitchen they installed a kerosene stove, a bread cupboard, and a square oak table from the Saturday-night auction. After two years, they wired the place; we still kept the kerosene lamps on top of the bread cupboard for emergencies. They hung cabinets and pasted wallpaper, and painted themselves out the kitchen door four Sundays in a row, painting the wood floor green, splattering it successively with red, yellow, and black, to echo Jackson Pollock's canvasses. (Until a few years before his death when my father tackled abstraction himself, he was suspicious of abstract painting, and this was his way of making fun of it.) They painted the fieldstone fireplace in the living room white. (We warmed our nightgowns before the fire, then ran to the unheated upstairs.) In the same room my mother whitewashed the dark pine paneling. They built closets in their bedroom and a desk below one window; from the other you could watch hummingbirds breakfasting on the bee-balm hedge. After my younger sister was born, my parents partitioned three odd-shaped rooms upstairs and built a tiny half-bath to forestall nighttime trips down the crooked stairs. Country plumbing plagued my father, and in time they installed a septic tank and new pipes for the kitchen sink. The leaky glassed-in porch, where I lost myself in the player piano and an illustrated book of Gilbert and Sullivan songs, was expanded into a family room. At the back door, my father laid a patio of flagstones that shone black and treacherous after a rain. I cut my knee on a sprawl across the flagstones and still have the patio dirt in my scar. The vegetable garden was excavated and replaced by a blue swimming pool filled with icy spring water. Their building projects punctuated my first thirteen years as naturally as snow tunnels, leaf piles, and mud in the spring.

They bought the place from a couple named Marchand, Julia and Gustave, and Mrs. Marchand wrote letters for years to send news and acknowledge each semi-annual mortgage payment. My parents paid $6,250 at 4½ percent interest for seven acres, the six-room house, two-car garage, chicken house, goat shed, and the school house one field away on the corner of Flockstown and Naughright roads.

The chickens left their feed and feathery smell behind in the chicken-house. My parents threw in there anything that could endure the feathers, dust, and the weather that came in through cracks in the windows and walls. The goat shed became our playhouse, and it collected yellow-jacket nests in its eaves. One time my father rammed the lawnmower into it, probably in frustration because he could never get the grass close to the little house except with hand clippers, and he disturbed the yellow-jackets, who followed him in a stream as he ran for the house like a man in a cartoon. He was allergic to bee and wasp stings and might have died if they'd reached him. In our family we knew the dangers that stalked my father.

∾

Mostly, we were city people. We lived at 164 State Street in Brooklyn Heights. I viewed the passing world—trees, stone houses, and rattling trolleys on the street in front of Abraham & Strauss—from a prone position, framed by the hood of my baby carriage. It seems early to have a memory, but it must be authentic, for how else could I recall such a view? I hid behind the arm of the couch when I heard my father's footsteps on the stairs, and waited for him to find me.

My sister Valerie was three years older than I, and we shared a tiny room just off my parents' bedroom, meant to be a dressing room or maybe it was a space left over when the building was converted to apartments. The room was filled by two beds and two child-size wardrobes. On top of my wardrobe, a dim light in the shape of a goldfish saw me through the night. I would have given it up for pride when Valerie teased me about it, but I was afraid to fall asleep without it. This was the beginning of Valerie teaching me to be ashamed of calling attention to myself. I never knew when her scorn would surprise me out of whatever I was doing or feeling.

The apartment house in Brooklyn was four stories tall, with the apartments straddling the steep, carpeted stairs. When

I was six, my father changed jobs and we moved to Manhattan, to an apartment building twelve stories tall, set back from the street, the gloomy distance to the entrance door covered with an awning: 55 West Ninety-fifth Street. In the new apartment, Valerie had her own room. When Sarah was born, I shared a room with her. By making the living room into a study and bedroom, and using the adjoining dining-room as the living room and an office for Daddy, my parents captured a suite for themselves. My mother made slipcovers out of a gray, tweedy fabric, and she dressed the couch and the easy chair in them when the weather turned in the spring. (The couch lasted longer than the family, until 1995.) My father's paintings were hung along the hallway—an oil of the beach at Daytona, Florida; a watercolor of Provincetown, Massachusetts, sailboats in the harbor; the portrait of my mother. Valerie's bedroom was down the hall by the apartment door, too close to the front door, too far in my view from Mommy and Daddy. She kept a parakeet who died one day while we were at school.

The kitchen was more or less a trapezoid. The refrigerator was on one side of the doorless doorway, the broom closet on the other. On the left as you entered were the dish cabinets, drawers, and a counter in between. When we moved in, my father built a table that hung down from the end of the counter; when it was down, you couldn't reach the cabinets and, when it was up, there was barely room to pass. I sat just beyond the table and watched my mother cook, looking out to a view across the shadowed courtyard through the big window. Set into the wall below the window was a metal cabinet that I feared, where my mother stored her onions and garlic. If I ever opened it, I'd fall into the unknown, down to the bottom of the courtyard and beyond.

The steam pipe in the bathroom carried voices from the apartment below. When the elevator stopped at another floor, I caught the ragged end of familial conversation *(Later! I've got to! I told you already!)*, the rushed slamming of a door, and the startled look of the person who hadn't realized there was anyone there listening. In the mosaic-tiled halls, I saw umbrellas and boots, and caught glimpses of apartments through partially opened doors, and sometimes heard screams and arguments, clues to the interior life. I became all eyes and ears in the hallway and on the elevator. The outside world, harsh and full of fascination, began as soon as I opened our door.

∾

One day my mother left me in the apartment with my older sister. I went straight to the top drawer of my mother's dresser where she kept her stockings, underthings, and her jewelry box, a shallow rectangular wooden box that might once have held a carving set. I kept alert for the front door opening or my older sister discovering what I was doing. In a separate box, dark blue, rested a strand of pearls, her only jewelry of value. I opened the jewelry box and found, jumbled in with the costume pieces and my father's medals from summer camp, a wide band set with square stones in an unfamiliar palette I would later recognize as Southwestern (turquoise, carnelian, onyx). I forced the ring past the knuckle of the second finger on my right hand. I admired the ring, then tried to slip it off. It wouldn't budge. I sucked my finger. This did no good. My finger was beginning to swell and turn red. There was plenty of precedent in Grimm's fairy tales for such a calamity.

I had no choice. I went to Valerie who was in her room. She snorted and told me I was stupid, but she sprang into action, trying butter to ease the ring's journey, and when that failed ordering me to put my coat on. "We're going to the shoemaker," she said. I followed Valerie down the street and around the corner.

The shoemaker's shop was crowded not only with bags and boxes of shoes, but with religious calendars, medals, statues, and holy cards. He worked at his bench facing the window. His hands were stained with shoe polish and oils, and the heavy smell of oil and leather was the liveliest presence in the shop. Along one side of the shop were stalls with swinging wooden doors for customers to sit in their socks and wait, and a throne for those who wanted a shoeshine. The customers who waited seemed to have left the land of the living just by giving up their shoes. They read the paper or dozed or watched silently as their shoes were mended.

The shoemaker was reluctant to help. But, as Valerie pointed out, something had to be done, and fast. My finger was turning white in patches.

He gestured me back behind the counter where shoes were piled. Using a clipper that he might ordinarily have chosen for stubborn boots or heavy work shoes, he managed to slip one blade under the ring and then, telling me not to move, he snipped. The ring came apart neatly. He gathered up the stones and the ruined band and gave them to my sister. She couldn't pay him because she didn't have any money. He waved us out of there.

Until the moment that the ring snapped, I was sure that the shoemaker was going to cut off my finger.

⁓

On one side of our country house was an overgrown field, good for blueberries in the summer, and, on the other side of the field, the dusty schoolhouse where I played the organ, making it groan its few remaining notes. I read the sums and mottoes of the last class taught there, for the schoolhouse had closed so long before our ownership that the chalked numbers and letters couldn't be washed from the slates. Once or twice a summer, my father pushed the lawnmower up the road past the blueberry field to trim the high grass around the schoolhouse in case of a brush fire.

On the other side of our house was a brook and, beyond a wet field, the Downes's farm. By the end of a summer every daisy, tiger lily, and stray shoot of hay was as familiar as the dips and ruts of the dirt road we walked to the farm. We played almost daily with Hattie Downes, the farmer's daughter who was Valerie's age. Hattie was an only child and had the farm all to herself. The Holsteins, the hissing geese, the rope swing that hung in the big maple outside the kitchen window, the deep freezer like a tomb, were all hers, all year. I never wondered if I liked Hattie. She was there, as much a part of the country as the trees. She and I—not often Valerie—followed the brook under the road and into the woods, sometimes coming upon cows who looked up, surprised to see us.

Woods lay in back of our house. I went into the woods alone, on an old path to a spring which was covered by an iron, rusting cone. The path must have been worn when the spring was the water source for the house. If I stood on tiptoe and leaned my weight against the corroding metal I saw the water far below, the purest in the world and the coldest.

The small red wood-frame garage lay at the end of the driveway, crowded with my father's tools, the lawnmower and the roller that he used on molehills and other uneven spots, his canvases, his skis, our junk. Also stored in the garage were my father's paintings, his big wooden easel, and the wooden suitcase that held his oil paints. Before we were born, he had studied painting, but now he had no time for it.

Near the barn was an ancient apple tree where I had napped on a pink satin quilt, the quilt faded and dulled with washing and stained by sweet rotting apples. The danger in the

Laura Furman, New Jersey, age eight

sweetness was the small yellow bees that lodged deep in the brown flesh of the apples.

Along the lawn from garage to playhouse was a hump where the level of the lawn changed no more than four inches, marking the boundary between real lawn with soft grass and a field that had been cut over time into a prickly area resembling a lawn. The hump made a place to roll somersaults and when I grew dizzy I rested my head against its gentle slope. Beyond the tops of our trees, I looked for the center of the sky, and tried to read in the hieroglyphics of the clouds what my fate would be. I meant by that what story I would be heroine of, for I wanted to live a life that would make others look at me and say, There she is. I imagined that if ever it were required, I'd be brave.

In the country summers, we had our routine that we followed all week. We were free to wander in the morning while my mother worked on the house or cleaned or gardened or put up blueberry preserves, blackberry and grape jelly, pickled watermelon rinds and cucumbers with dill and garlic. We tried to crawl through the chicken doors to get into the chicken house. We had our swing set, the hammock for sleeping, rocking, and reading, and the tree it hung from to climb. The same tree had a swing that my father had made from a board and a length of rope. We played in the brook, tossing rocks sometimes at harmless water snakes, over Valerie's angry shouts, for she wanted to protect them.

A forsythia bush by the weathered picket fence at the front of the property formed another playhouse, and the ground it sheltered was smooth, except for the roots of the bush and the surrounding trees. It was my cave and I shared it sometimes with my sister or friends, or retreated there from them. The front porch had big Adirondack chairs but was tricky because the shingled walls that ran along the porch were filled with yellow-jacket nests. Sometimes they were disturbed by us, sometimes not. The hatch-door to the cellar steps was on the other end of the porch from the reading chairs. The walls of the cellar were old fieldstone and the cellar was cold in summer, warm in winter. The furnace was down there and wobbly shelves with jars. Eventually my father built shelves in the kitchen to hold the preserves my mother made over the summer. In front of the house a lawn sloped down to a snow fence and the forsythia cave. After dinner on summer nights we captured fireflies in glass jars and left them with a few blades of grass, hoping the holes punched in the tops of the jars would provide them air to live until morning.

After lunch we often drove to the Morgensterns' house, or the girls came to us. Dick and Faith Morgenstern were friends of my parents, she a large, smooth, pretty woman, and he a dark, muscled man with a short temper. He manufactured children's clothing for a living, and collected vintage cars with running boards and rumble seats. Their daughters, Annie and Beatrice, were our friends. Beatrice was closer to my age but still a little older, and Annie and Valerie were the same age. It was like having three older sisters, though the Morgenstern girls tolerated me better than Valerie did. Faith and my mother were close, and gave each other time off by arranging when we girls would play together. We swam in their pond for hours, one mother or another or both by the side in bathing suits and sunglasses. I believed, against all reason, that the bottom of the pond was entirely coated with dried-out duck poop, from the large family of ducks that also swam on the pond. If I touched bottom and felt sharp peaks of duck poop (probably rocks), I'd scramble to the surface.

I didn't swim very well for all the hours I spent in the water. My father tried to teach all of us and succeeded with Valerie, but I refused to put my face in the water and despite his pantomime from shore never learned from him how to swim. I didn't like putting my face into the darkness, where I invariably choked, so my association with darkness became airlessness. It was many years before I caught on that I should gulp in air when I turned my head and expel it when I pressed my face back into the water.

When our lips were blue, we were told to come out, and we lay on the green banks of the pond, wrapped in towels rough from the clothesline.

At the Morgensterns' I learned to ride a two-wheeler bike. Valerie, Annie, and Beatrice took me to the lawn at the spot where it began its long slope down to the pond. They positioned me on the bike, steadied me, and let me go. "Steer, steer," they ordered, then, "Brake, brake." Riding my own baby-blue two-wheeler when I got it, pretending it was my horse and I, a cowgirl, riding past the schoolhouse and back home—this was the pleasure and freedom they gave me by teaching me to ride. Still, I never dared to go past a certain point on the road, stopped not by my mother's prohibitions but by my own reluctance to venture far from home.

❧

Once my mother took me along when she met her friend Evelyn Vargas for lunch. Evelyn was a dancer, then in *Kismet* on Broadway, and Paco, her husband, was a documentary film director. Our families got together in the city and the country. In the country they lived in a large Dutch stone house that was cool, summer and winter. The place was eccentric and beautiful, and they camped out in it flamboyantly. I loved their mess and their sense of playing house. The children were more serious than the parents in that family.

Lunch was in a French restaurant in midtown, somewhere in the West Fifties, a simple place, a few steps down from street level. My mother had broad, hand-cut noodles with a chicken liver sauce. The color of the sauce was roux-brown and it coated the white noodles. It was memorable to be included in a time of two women friends together.

When I lived in New York in my twenties and worked in midtown, I looked for the restaurant where my mother and I ate with Evelyn, sure that I would recognize it. It didn't occur to me until recently that perhaps the restaurant was gone.

∼

When we drove to visit family friends in Larchmont and New Rochelle on winter weekends when we weren't in New Jersey, the suburban houses we passed looked blank and without mystery. The post-war developments on Long Island were, in the sameness of the houses, a terrible exposure of the simple need for shelter, and the houses looked lonelier than even the most isolated farmhouse I'd seen on the ride to or from the country, a farmhouse lit and glimpsed across a snow-covered night field. Even the big houses in Larchmont and New Rochelle were oddly isolated, though closer together than the country houses they often resembled. Houses were like boxes, standing alone.

Apartments were different, for they were drawers—stuffed, active, unknowable from without, filled with detailed lives and different ways of doing things, even in apartments with identical layouts. After we moved to 55 West Ninety-fifth Street, I developed an interest in what went on inside drawers when they were shut. I jerked them open to try to catch a glimpse of the life inside but never succeeded in seeing anything but the jumble I'd left of clothes or pens and papers .

I feel like that still. If I open the drawers of memory just right, if I remember the places I lived and knew, if I can put the places into words, then I may understand the life inside.

∾

My piano teacher, a big-bosomed German woman who smelled of perspiration and cologne, lived in the apartment next door to us, but one floor down. Her apartment was filled with furniture, and every table and shelf covered with framed photographs, albums, and music. She gave lessons in the first room off a long hallway, a small room stuffed with an upright and a bench. Since we had no piano, I was invited to practice in her apartment, and when it was practice time, the halls of the building seemed cold, the distance too great from our apartment. Once I was there—once through the halls, the elevator, the wait at her door, past the greeting, her Kleenex which she always kept knobbed up and tucked into her sleeve, her cologne—I found out anew that I wasn't any good at piano. I looked from the notes and black marks on the sheet of music to the black and white keyboard and back again, seeking a connection, and I found none.

∾

In an apartment two floors down but with a layout identical to the piano teacher's, Bill and Madeline Stern lived with their daughter Lucy who was about my younger sister's age. Bill was a medical resident. Madeline was in graduate school and she often needed to be at class or doing research for her thesis. Madeline had had polio as a girl, and I associated the polio with her crackly voice and her quick deep laugh. She always seemed glad to see me. I baby sat for Lucy long after I stopped taking piano lessons, and I wondered that in the same small room two floors below where I'd been tortured by my inadequacy and lack of talent, slept a freckled girl with straight hair and long floppy bangs. While she slept, I listened to Woody

Guthrie albums and the Weavers, looking at the gaunt face of Woody when he was young.

Madeline finished her degree, and Bill his residency. They had another baby, a boy, and moved across the Hudson to a pretty house in Nyack. I went across the river to visit the Sterns but I felt shy there, and out of place with the new family of four, although I recognized and felt at home with some of their things—an old dresser crammed with clothes that had blocked the hallway in the old apartment, now empty in the guest room, painted bright yellow to match the roses on the wallpaper. They were entirely settled in their new house, and I wondered that apartment people could so easily change to house people. The big, airy rooms of the house, the screened-in porch, the dark suburban night, told me that I was a relic from the Sterns' city life.

∼

When our first apartment became too crowded we moved to another apartment in the same building. The move up a few floors and over a few hundred yards made as much difference as changing towns would have for another child. After the move strangers took over the space where we had lived, and the life we'd lived there vanished to make room for a new family to exist.

In the new apartment Sarah and I still shared a room. In order to make the one room more like two, my mother balanced folding shutters of near ceiling height between our matching beds and dressers. The balance wasn't perfect. The shutters wobbled when my mother changed the sheets on our beds and cleaned the room. They tilted daily and threatened to fall. Sarah stared through a slit as I lay on my bed, reading or dreaming, and I'd feel her eyes on me and explode. Or I'd pretend not to notice until she tipped the shutter toward me. More than any other of our city rooms, even the old kitchen, our bedroom was packed like a suitcase. My parents had a bedroom down the hall, and Valerie had the maid's room off the kitchen, down the hall and far from the rest of us. She and Sarah were a team, and I was at war with them. I didn't mind as much being excluded from their play as being ridiculed for whatever I did or said.

I began to take refuge in the bathroom that we all shared. I used to search my mother's medicine cabinet and examine her lipstick and loose powder, her fine sandpaper mitt for rubbing the hair from her upper lip, her bottle of Mary Chess perfume. Sometimes I'd spread the bath mat on the cool tile floor and lie on it, staring up. The bathroom overlooked the open shaft between our building and the next, and the light was gray and dusky all day long, an evening tone I identify as New York light.

∿

In summer, my father spent weekdays in the city and returned to the country and us on Friday night. His arrival spelled the end of the ordinary week, the end of pleasingly similar days. He would call in the morning to let my mother know which train he was catching. My mother spent Friday cleaning the house and getting ready for him, and before the afternoon was out, we made the winding drive past Long Valley to meet him at the train.

He took the train from Manhattan to a pretty village called Gladstone. If we got to Gladstone early, we had to cool our heels staring down the track. When I read *Anna Karenina*, I imagined Anna's final scene in the Gladstone station. Descending from the train, my father was always rumpled and hot-looking in his seersucker suit, his summer hat, the *Times* and his briefcase in one hand, the other arm free to catch us. In the moment before he saw us he looked exhausted, as if he carried the terrible hot city on his shoulders.

Our life was different when my father was there, the air filled with the noise of the lawn mower or his power saw, and if we went anywhere together, he drove the car. I was aware, and I'm sure Valerie was more so, that after we went to sleep they became other and separate selves.

Social life was also different on weekends, because it included the other men, drinking, and meals out at one house or another. My parents went for drinks to Tommy and Dodie Frank's, and took us along. The Franks had a cocker spaniel I liked, though I wasn't much used to dogs, and I was allowed to go outside and wander or even go into Tommy's studio and look at his worktable and his paintings in progress. When friends came to us, my father grilled chicken, and the grown-ups tried to leave their glasses in drink holders that were stabbed into the ground and never stayed upright, but never fell.

I could barely imagine that the city existed while we were absent from it, but when my father spent his vacation weeks at the country house, my mother went into the city on occasion to get her hair cut or for a dentist appointment, or perhaps just to have a day to herself when she could move quickly, unencumbered by children. Once she took me into the city with her while Sarah stayed with Daddy, and when we returned—driving ourselves back from Gladstone in the car we'd left in the station that morning—we found that he'd cut Sarah's hair. When we'd left she had light pretty locks all over her head, now it was close to her head with bangs, the cut he gave me and Valerie. Daddy had run out of ways to entertain the small girl and chose the haircut in desperation. Sarah's hair grew back darkened and thicker, no longer baby hair.

On Saturday we all made the trip to Hackettstown to stock

up for the week. When I was old enough, while my mother went to the grocery store and my father to the hardware store, I was allowed to explore the five and dime myself and look at the store windows along the main street, so pristine compared to New York. We bought our shoes at a store with a cardboard cutout in the window of Buster Brown and his little dog, and we put our feet inside a tall x-ray machine to be sure our new shoes fit right. At the jewelry store she bought a gold bracelet for me and had a charm inscribed "June 1957", the date of my graduation from elementary school. There was a luncheonette where we met up to eat sandwiches and sundaes if my father said yes, and a paint store where my mother and I spent days looking for wallpaper for my room. We chose a pattern of silver and white ballerinas on a blue-gray background which later she hung like a mural, covering most but not all of the longest wall.

On Sunday morning we drove down the road to the general store so that my parents could buy the *Times*. Valerie and I were each given a nickel, sometimes a dime, and we were allowed to go behind the glass cabinet of penny candy, slide open the big door, and reach in for what we wanted. We often got an ice cream cone, and senselessly bit off the bottom of the cone, then raced to finish before the ice cream melted through and made a mess in the car.

∽

On Monday mornings in July and August, even before the sun had cleared the woods, my father stood at the deep end of the swimming pool, poised to dive. At the far end of the lawn the blue concrete rectangle that had replaced the vegetable garden was filled with spring water as clear and cold as ice. Propelled by the force of the dive, he swam the length of the pool underwater, and when he emerged his arms were still outstretched, his hands together and pointed ahead, as if he might be preparing to dive again. Once out of the pool, he began walking down the broken concrete path to the house, through the dew-wet lawn, wrapped in the towel he'd left in wait.

I say he swam but rather he dove, first standing arms upstretched and streamlined, pausing for longer than the simple dive required. He hesitated because the morning was cold and the water he was about to enter frigid, but the hesitation gave his stance a meditative quality as if he were completing prayers before immersing himself in holy water.

He swam right before my mother drove him to Gladstone to catch the early train with the other commuting men in their seersucker suits and bowties. He smelled of his starched cotton shirt and fresh newspaper ink. His cheek was shaven smooth.

∾

When I try to imagine what the long weeks between weekends were like for my mother, it is hard to push past my own happiness at the simplicity of the days. She had always worked, first to get out of Atlanta, then to come to New York and live independently, and surely she wanted sometimes to be with adults, not constantly to cook, clean, and care for kids.

One summer day, Mommy was serving lunch to Valerie and me at the big square oak table in the kitchen. Valerie and Mommy were quarreling and I reached for my milk. My hand hit the glass and the milk spilled all over the table and dribbled down between the leaves to the floor, coating the table leg. She slapped me for the first and only time, and I jumped up and went into the bathroom, closing the door behind me. Her injustice, more than the pain, shocked me. I enjoyed being her favorite and her unique slap represented a demotion. Both my mother and father hit Valerie every once in a while on the car trips to and from the city when sometimes both would turn around in the front seat—he driving, she riding shotgun—losing their tempers simultaneously in some choreography of parenthood, and slap her. Now, the invisible order of our family places had shifted, and I was in Valerie's role, however temporarily. My mother stood outside the door and apologized to me. She'd thought I'd spilled the milk on purpose, she said. She must have feared that something important between us was broken for good.

❧

When he was growing up in the twenties in Bensonhurst, a leafy section of Brooklyn, my father set up his easel and painting table on the screened-in porch and his brothers were instructed to leave him alone. *Sylvan is painting.* He worked in oil paints with their solid smell and the sharpness of turpentine on his rags, painting trees and houses, a self-portrait with a pipe. He was the first son, smart, destined to be a college boy. His father Louis came from the heroic generation, as Sylvan called it, immigrants who came with nothing and made businesses, families, made college graduates. My father hadn't always been the oldest. His sister Janet had died of blood poisoning, the result of a scratch on her nose that had become infected, the kind of thing parents now prevent with antibacterial cream sold over the counter.

Slow down, he'd tell us, angrily. *Watch where you're going. Watch out.* And when we were hurt, he behaved as if we'd endangered ourselves willfully.

He never spoke of Janet's death, though it was not a kept secret since I learned of it. He told me that my grandmother became depressed and never really recovered from her daughter's death.

In a file labeled "Cemetery" my father kept papers pertaining to the Furman family plot in Mount Judah Cemetery

Sylvan Furman, and self-portrait

in Brooklyn. He didn't attend the annual meetings of the cemetery owners but he faithfully signed the proxy form, mailed it back, and kept the stub, initialed and dated. There is a stack of these in the file. The oldest document is from 1937, detailing a bequest from my great-grandfather David Furman, a member of the Brith Abraham lodge, to his wife Ettie and his son, Louis M., my grandfather, both of Brooklyn. By the time David died in 1941, my grandfather was living in Daytona Beach. He sent a change of address telegram to the cemetery office and wrote that he was "obliged to move to Florida…, due to illness in the family." I hear his uprootedness in the "obliged" and wonder that he felt compelled to explain the reason for his change of address—business failure as much as his youngest son's asthma—in a telegram that he paid for by the word.

A family problem developed after my grandfather's brother, Morris, was buried in the family plot. Initially, when my great-grandfather and grandfather had bought the plot, Morris declined to share in the cost, saying he'd be cremated when the time came. Now my grandfather asked my father to act as a go-between to secure Morris' share of perpetual care from his heirs, preferably to be paid in a large sum at once. He wrote to my father: "Grandpa and I bought the plot about 30 years ago when we were still young, and did not expect to die & money was plentiful."

My father spoke to his cousin, relayed the details of a proposed solution, and then, cautioning his father against anger, he wrote: "Even if there is a matter of principle involved, it seems to me that there are so many other problems in life that this is not a major one and is not worth the expenditure of a lot of worry and energy. As you and Ma have often said—'abee gesund.' "

This Yiddish expression translates as, "As long as you're

healthy," a phrase my father used often both to put things in perspective and to keep troubles at bay.

My father wanted to be left alone all his life. He wanted to be left alone to paint, to read, and to listen to music. He might have been a painter, had he not been the first son in an immigrant family, not married and fathered children. In the last fifteen years of his life, he studied painting again and took up etching, free at last, and though he reproached himself for not working harder, he was more productive than he knew. He loved the solitary act of reading—books, magazines, *The New York Times*, the back of cereal boxes. He began to lose his hearing in his sixties and insisted that a hearing aid wouldn't help his type of hearing loss. At the end he found a hearing aid that helped although it squealed and squeaked and failed him. With earphones, he could hear music perfectly, and often he lay back in his recliner to listen to the radio or to his tapes. If one of us came into the room, we'd be able to watch him for several minutes before he noticed us. Deafness suited him in those moments, cutting him off from life but leaving him music. At other times, of course, deafness isolated him, and he got a new expression on his face in his last years, of eagerness to be included and to know what was going on around him.

∽

When I ate at other houses, I was confused because nowhere was like home. Was this supposed to be better than my mother's cooking or was hers superior? What was food supposed to be like?

The dishes I liked best, aside from matzoh ball soup at Passover, were corn on the cob from our garden and lamb chops.

In the country we picked corn from the garden only when the water in the big pot began to boil. We shucked the ears onto newspapers outside on the flagstone patio, rushed the raw corn into the boiling water, then ate it dripping with butter and glistening with salt. We held the corn on two-pronged plastic holders that were themselves shaped like ears of corn, and we rolled the corn on a stick of butter, leaving silk and stray kernels that we'd find for days. The corn holders never quite worked and we never had quite enough of them to go around, so often I ate with one holder slipping in my buttered and salted hand while the other hand grasped the corn itself.

Once my mother made brains, though she and my father were the only ones who enjoyed the dish. I tried a forkful and quit. Valerie refused to eat any. Maybe my mother wasn't being sophisticated. Maybe they cooked brains, breaded and sautéed, in Georgia.

When my mother made blintzes, she covered the Formica and metal kitchen table with clean dishcloths. She mixed the thin batter, then heated a cast-iron sauté pan. She added no shortening to the pan because it was so well seasoned that it didn't need it. (My father stood guard over our battery of cast-iron pans, warning me always to wipe and never to wash, never to leave one soaking in water.) My mother ladled a small amount of batter onto the heated pan—it always looked like too little to me—swirled the heavy pan to distribute the batter evenly, then replaced the pan on the burner to let the pancake cook. She picked up the pan that cradled the just-right blintz, swept it over to the table, and in one gesture turned the pan upside down and dropped the blintz flat onto the waiting cloth. This worked most of the time, and when a blintz tore or folded over, I got to eat the mistakes.

She filled the blintz with a cottage-cheese mixture or grape jelly, sometimes blueberry preserves she'd made herself, folding over the edges of the blintzes as carefully as if she were planning to stack and store them forever.

❧

Once I began going to school, I hurried along the city streets, aware of the men sitting on stoops speaking Spanish who watched me as I passed, and tried not to collide with packs of roller-skating boys. The dark Irish bar on the corner of Ninety-fifth and Columbus had neon green shamrocks twinkling in its black glass windows. A square column divided the tiled entrance space, and the door was nearly always open to an interior as black as night and smelling of spilled beer and something else, cardboard or stale popcorn. The bar looked like a hole asking to be fallen into. I never went in, and now it's gone, the whole block is gone.

Next door was the hardware store, crowded with necessary, unexciting goods, and next to it the small grocery store we dashed into for one or two items at a time. Sometimes we went to the butcher across Columbus, down from the A&P, for special quality meat. Once a week my mother shopped at the A&P across Columbus, where there was a coffee machine that ground beans into a pungent powder. Dogs were leashed outside the store, and sometimes strollers. I disliked waiting outside with the dogs. The street was too large a place to be without my mother. I might be swept along and not be able to return to her.

She took me with her when she shopped out of the neighborhood in the big department stores, Best & Co. on Fifth Avenue, S. Klein's in Union Square. She hunted for bargains in a trance. If I dawdled and she moved on, or if she became too absorbed in sorting slowly through the neat racks on the muted floors of Best & Co. or the piles of clothing on tables in the uncarpeted, undivided space of Klein's or I wandered off, I knew what to do: go to the cashier and tell her I was lost, tell her my name. And after a while an announcement was made over the loudspeaker, calling for the mother of a lost child. My mother appeared, clothes flung over her arm, looking flushed and worried. I had dreams of being claimed by women who lied and said they were my mother, of not being heard when I protested or asked for help.

Around the corner on Ninety-sixth Street was the beauty shop. My father, who usually cut our hair, said each time that haircutting was just like sculpture and he trimmed my bangs so they went up on one side. If he tried to correct the angle, my bangs ended up at my hairline. I thought that if only I went to the beauty parlor I would be transformed and look just like the cardboard window display of a blonde angel-curled baby. My mother got her hair cut, not very often, on Fifth Avenue and Forty-second Street, in a little shop above a cigar store. After she died, I went there a few times but I couldn't be sure if the hairdresser was the same one or if he would remember her if I asked. I began to wonder if the shop might have changed hands, then I stopped going there.

Early on, my mother and I walked down our street to the school bus stop on Central Park and Ninety-fifth, in dim light with rain hanging in the air and in bright cold, the wind chilling my face. My mother stood too close to me, and often found a smudge on my face, took a fuzzy Kleenex from her pocket, one she'd blotted her lipstick on so that the red outline of her mouth lingered. She wet the Kleenex on her tongue and rubbed at my face. If my nose was running, she held the tissue against my face and commanded, "Blow." Now when I blot my lipsticked mouth on Kleenex, I smell my mother and feel her wetness that rested on my cheek like a birthmark.

Sometimes my mother and I walked down the same block not to wait for the school bus but to turn and walk north and cross east to get to the playground. On the swings, slide, and sandbox, I lost myself as I did in the country, except when I looked up to be sure my mother was on the bench where I'd last seen her. A great division came when my mother said that I was old enough to play in the park across Ninety-sixth Street while she watched from a park bench, although I was not to go past the bridle path. Later still I was let loose to venture beyond the bridle path, to run and play with friends in the tunnels and paths beyond my mother's sight. We found empty bottles in rumpled paper bags in the tunnels or held our noses to keep out the smell of urine, but sometimes the tunnels were a clean mystery we rushed through, pausing a second in the middle, the scary part where water ran down the brown stones, as if we'd reached the center of the New York earth.

∿

My second grade teacher was a large woman who wore lace dickeys over her long dresses. Once in a while, she raged at us in a mad way that I recognized later when I saw *King Lear*. I was careful not to laugh too loud or to do anything to attract her attention, whichever way the wind was blowing.

One day the class got a new shipment of Little Golden Books, from the Board of Education, the teacher said, and she warned us to be careful with them. Our hands should be clean before we touched them. We shouldn't tear them. We shouldn't spill anything on them. We shouldn't write in them. The Little Golden Books I had at home received the very treatment she warned against. The pages of my *Poky Little Puppy* were limp and the corners of the cardboard cover turned up and separated into layers of cardboard and glossy cover stock. It wasn't contempt that drove me to color and write in books I loved, but the feeling that they were part of me.

I had one of the new books to myself and was reading it carefully, prissily, when I forgot myself, something I tried never to do at school, and I became involved in the story. I heard an awful sound. I'd ripped a page. One finger had stayed on the book while my other hand turned the page. The teacher pounced and screamed. I'd ruined the book. I must pay for it. Penniless like all children, I cried, adding humiliation to fear, unable to imagine coming up with such a sum.

The next day my mother came to school in her red tweed suit with black buttons. When I saw her in the classroom with my teacher I wanted her to leave because I thought the teacher would harm her. They finished their conversation, and my mother went on to the principal's office.

By the following week I was Intellectually Gifted, in a class I hadn't been placed in to start with, and though I never quite felt I belonged, I was happier there. As long after as the next school year, when I passed the door to my original second-grade classroom, I remembered my pride and fear at seeing my mother at the door in her red tweed suit.

I had been afraid of school from my first day in Kindergarten at P. S. 75 when I heard the heavy door slam behind my mother as she left me there. I assumed my mother was as afraid of school as I was. After she succeeded in rescuing me from the second-grade teacher, my mother was able to leave, and I imagined the relief she felt when she was outside the door.

In the days before Sarah was born, there was no place like our apartment during the day when my father was at work and Valerie at school, when no one was at home but my mother and me. Being at home in the middle of the day still feels like a gift. Once I started going to school it was a gift bestowed only by sickness. Some of my happiest memories are of chicken pox, sore throats, fevers unattached to names. Mornings when I was home sick, I slept on and off, listening to my mother cleaning the apartment—vacuuming, dusting, sweeping, washing dishes—until even in my sick room I smelled the harsh familiar detergents and polishes. The quiet in the apartment was not just silence but peace and the ease between my mother and me. At noon, we'd have lunch at the fold-out table in the kitchen or she'd bring me a tray in bed. I returned to bed, grateful to be there again, and slept on and off until late in the afternoon when my sole possession of my mother would end.

∽

I had places all over the apartment to read in, and I devoured all books, Nancy Drew, *Arabian Nights*, anything with a story. In the house in New Jersey, I read in a hammock strung between the chicken house and a big elm, in my bed upstairs with its chenille cover getting wet from the rain at the open window, and at night with the moths throwing themselves madly against the screen. I read in the car driving up to the country, and often I looked up to see that the sun was setting and we were halfway there.

Once my mother died, I had a mission and reading was never the same. At home, on the bus, waiting for the dentist, anywhere I was, I had a book and I read. So long as I had my book with me, I was never alone and I was never myself, living past my mother, in the city, going home to the maid who wanted to go home to her own, stuck with my sisters who, it seemed, lived to scorn me, and my father who wasn't much there. My mission was to search for a life that I might want to live. I tore through books looking for clues, for I was sure that stories were a road map, and while I read, I had the hope that I should be so lucky and find my ticket out.

∽

A drugstore stood on the southeast corner of Ninety-sixth Street and Columbus Avenue, and occupied most of the first floor of an apartment building which fronted on Ninety-sixth Street. At the entrance to the drugstore was a white mosaic floor with numbers in a contrasting color, once indigo, and a black border. The tiles were hexagonal, like those on our bathroom floor. The tile of the entrance continued inside, thousands of small white hexagons set inside the dark border that emphasized the squareness of the space, at odds with the long soda fountain and, opposite, the glass cases displaying cosmetics and perfumes, the cash register, and, elevated, the pharmacist's laboratory.

My sharpest memory of the drugstore fades when I look at it, a heat oasis on a summer highway. One day I went into the pharmacy and saw something I wanted to give my mother, a bottle of perfume. It was a drugstore object far beyond the reach of my allowance, then probably between a nickel and fifteen cents per week, which was sufficient for spending but not for saving. The gift was unlike our family. It was bright, new, and a little flashy. We wore hand-me-down clothes and drove the same car forever. My parents made things last and always shopped for a bargain. My father's income was stretched to the limit by the apartment in the city and the house and seven acres in the country. I was aware of the economies that ran us, and the vigilance to money-spending in any and every amount that told me that our lives cost money. Presents were given for Chanukah, for Christmas (which we celebrated with a decorated tree), and for birthdays, but not in the course of an ordinary day.

I asked the pharmacist if I could have the perfume for my mother who was sick. I told him I didn't have any money but that I would, somehow, pay him back. The pharmacist wrapped the perfume neatly, and I gave it to her, knowing even as I did that this wasn't going to work out. Then I had to go around the corner again and tell the druggist that I had lied. My mother was not sick. I'd made a silly gesture, imitating the gestures of the soap operas I loved to listen to on the radio.

When real drama came to our family, we pretended that everything was normal, and that was our form of theatre.

∾

Three times a week, I went after school to take ballet with Madame Mordkin. Our second apartment was on the same side of the building as Madame's. She was the widow of Mikhail Mordkin, one of Anna Pavlova's partners. The walls of the dressing room were covered with stage photographs of Mordkin and the incomparable Pavlova whose feet ended in perfect sharp points. Madame was short and broad, dressed in black from head to foot, and imperious. She screamed at us, at the pianist (another elderly exile), at anything that moved in her studio. She stamped her foot and beat time on the floor with a stick taller than she was. She screamed in French and Russian, not often in English.

Perhaps I took ballet lessons from her because she and my mother struck up a friendship in the hall or the elevator. In any case, for several years, I walked up West End Avenue from P. S. 75 to the Master Institute on One Hundred and Third Street and Riverside Drive where Madame Mordkin had her ballet studio. The studio and dressing room smelled of rosin and talcum powder. The costumes we used for our recital version of *Swan Lake* came from Pavlova's troupe, the heavy tulle skirts, sharp caps, the hand-painted silver wings hanging from our waists, and strapless bodices whose bones cut into our flesh. There were photographs in the dressing room of Pavlova, Mordkin, and other Russian dancers of the twenties and thirties. I recognized the costumes and tried to imitate the dancers' poses.

In the mirror-lined practice room, with the pianist pounding out Chopin, Madame Mordkin taught us the rudiments of ballet, ballet French, and exile. On the street she looked like any other old West Side lady, square, short, and vaguely old-fashioned. In her studio, dressed in a long black skirt, special soft shoes, and a black blouse, holding the stick in her hand with which she kept time by pounding the floor and which she threatened to hit us with when we were dense, she was something out of another country and time as well as the eternal world of dance. By screaming, she meant to turn us from American schoolgirls into serious conservatory students. She tried to imbue us with her tradition. Once in a while she would correct a position with her stick or her hands, and through touch communicated her grasping fury and her passionate involvement. I was convinced that I would be a dancer, and I loved the hard work of it, stretching and distorting my body, then breaking from the barre to progress across the floor or to find my center and twirl in multiple pirouettes. I remembered all the combinations Madame Mordkin taught. I earned her praise, for I had what Madame called elevation. When I leaped, I stayed in the air for longer than I would have thought possible, suspended and still for a moment before gravity took over. That moment of suspended flight, I flattered myself, was my true self, a glimpse of a great future. What I glimpsed in Madame Mordkin was the grip of a great past on a woman struggling to survive in an unkind present.

My parents agreed that I might also take an Adult Intermediate class that met in the evening if I came home with Madame Mordkin. I was the only child in the evening class; the others were grown women and Madame Mordkin screamed less than in the children's classes. She was easier on me in the Intermediate class, showing off my elevation to the older women who had more to carry upward.

How are you going to be a dancer if—you don't turn out properly, you can't turn more times in pirouette, you don't keep your chin up (the spine follows the head), you can't point your toes more? In ballet, as I would later find in Latin, there was a pleasurable and systematic language to be learned, and I watched the recital dances grow logically from the barre exercises. The performances, however, were only to be endured. It wasn't pleasure I felt when performing, more like uncomfortable ecstasy.

After class, I changed into street clothes and went down to Madame Mordkin's private dressing room, a tiny room filled with costumes needing repair or alteration, sheet music, more stage photographs, and Madame, short, heavy, not quite ready to leave. She sat before her mirror, the vanity littered with crumpled-up papers and open boxes of face powder and sticky stage makeup. Her voice, which carried so well across the studio, was not lowered much in conversation, though in all other ways she changed from the powerful teacher to an old lady with bad feet whom I had to help the whole tedious way home. I imagined that the people we passed on Broadway and the other passengers on the cross-town bus—which we took from Broadway to Columbus, two long uphill blocks—stared at us and wondered who we could possibly be. She had style and pride, I see now, to put on her lipstick and powder for the short trip back to Ninety-fifth Street.

∽

My father skated gracefully, a scarf wound around his neck, pipe clenched between his teeth, his hands clasped behind him like a Dutchman in an etching. In New Jersey he took me skating on a country pond that wound around islands of bare trees and twiggy shrubs. Unlike perfectly smooth city ice, country ice had to be watched for bumps and pockets where the wind had frozen a wave. Most people stayed near the bank, and I skated around the bend where there was no one in sight, going as far as I could under the snowburdened frozen trees, the birds moving with me, ending at a wall of snow the plow had left on the ice. Beyond, rabbits left their footprints.

In the city I skated at Wollman Memorial Skating Rink, the real heart of the park, far from its western and eastern boundaries, south of my usual playing spots. To get to the skating rink, my friends and I walked through the park or took the bus down Central Park West and walked east through the park. It was a serious excursion, one I made in the winter as regularly as I danced.

City skating was organized and more of a group activity than the country variety. However many people were on the pond's ice, we could go our own way, in groups, couples, or solo. In the city, everyone circled in one direction so that the mass of skaters seemed linked like the cars of a train as they moved around and around. Rowdy boys darted in and out of the skaters, and there was an unspoken agreement that the rink would be divided like a target, with the least experienced on the outside and the bull's eye reserved for the figure skaters. Looking back it seems that everyone skated but my mother.

One winter weekend, my father, Valerie, and I drove to Hunter, New York, to meet my father's old friend Nat Morgenstern and his sons for skating at Nat's cabin on a lake in the Catskills. Nat was a jovial man who, like his brother Dick and his father before him, manufactured children's clothing. He had a bigger collection of antique cars than his brother and a house in Westchester that we visited some Sundays. The cabin was closed up for the winter. The plumbing was off, and mothballs and newspapers covered the beds. The lake was big and flat, leading to small hills at the edge, an open winter landscape, defined by the difference in white and shadow, more rugged terrain than the pond in New Jersey.

Someone had cleared an area for us to skate on, and I sat on a log to put on my skates. I walked awkwardly to the ice. My father was off skating. I headed out alone. The ice looked smooth from the shore but it was rough and gave me an idea of what winter was really like to freeze the ripples on the lake. I hunched over like a racer and let my arms swing from side to side. It was a bright day and the glare of the sun off the ice and snow was blinding. Squinting through a veil of lashes, I wondered, as I wondered when I swam, where the center was and how far I could get before I had to turn back. It didn't seem that I would ever have to stop. Along with the sun on the snow, the bumps on the ice, there was a cold, strong wind out in the open, away from the break of pine trees and the cabin. One minute I was skating, arms working, the next I was in blackness.

When I came around I was inside the cabin, lying on a bed which was covered with newspapers. The cabin was dim and cold, and figures hovered over the bed—Nat, my father, my sister, one of the Morgenstern boys. I heard a noise from them, the chatter of relief. Don't move, someone said. I'd been knocked out cold. Being in the blackness, not remembering anything, these were signs of concussion, my father later explained. My memory ends at a feeling of nausea and an echo in my head. A gust of wind had knocked me over, I was told. Or I'd tripped on a bump in the ice.

I had the feeling when I opened my eyes in the cabin, that any amount of time might have passed. It might have been years and mine the sleep of Snow White or Sleeping Beauty. Anything might have happened while I slept. There was both terror and pleasure in the feeling that I'd lost time. Some mornings I wake with the same feeling, in the hope or fear that I might be a child again, taking for granted my mother's presence.

∾

Valerie was already going to Hunter College High School, an

all-girls' school from seventh through twelfth grades, run by the Board of Higher Education, only one indication of its superiority. We'd heard a rumor that you had to have an IQ of 135 before you were allowed even to take the test, and this impressed us in the days when the IQ measurement was gold.

On a rainy day I went by cab with a classmate and her mother across town and down Lexington Avenue to Hunter for the admissions examination. My mother must have stayed home with Sarah, who was then four. I loved taking cabs. Being out on a school day made the exam into a holiday, one that would end when the cab ride did. The cab was a Checker with jump seats that the other girl and I took, and the windshield wipers went back and forth in a regular, lugubrious rhythm. She began to hum the Toreador song from *Carmen* in time with the wipers, then I joined in. We started as the cab headed east across Central Park and continued as it rolled downhill through the wet and darkened stone tunnel.

The taxi ride to Hunter traced the route that I would take to school for the next six years: through the entrance to the stone-walled park where on the left was our playground, and on the right the unenclosed park; the crosstown ride during which I envied the peaceful trees that didn't have to go to school, then downtown on Lexington Avenue, a street jammed with shops and people. During that first ride the still wintry park was soaked, and in the gray northern light the trunks of the trees, the rough stones of the tunnels, the empty benches shone. The shine was something like the shine of sky, apple tree, barn, green lawn—the shine of the country.

Hunter occupied a Gothic castle on Lexington Avenue between Sixty-eighth and Sixty-ninth streets, and I got to know every inch of the building by the time I graduated. When I was a junior, my friends and I used to sneak up to the top floor and climb out onto a tiny section of the roof, looking over the parapets to Lexington Avenue below. We ate lunch, smoked cigarettes, and sometimes sang. Once someone brought wine and we felt very decadent returning to afternoon classes with a whiff of wine in our mouths.

My first year at Hunter I was thrown by leaving the neighborhood for school, and in the morning I worried about leaving the apartment late, because I couldn't find clothes to wear, and missing the cross-town bus. I stood on the corner of Ninety-sixth and Lexington, trying to decide as the minutes passed whether to take the subway which was always packed at that hour or to wait for the less-crowded bus. When I arrived at Hunter, I worried that I would go to the wrong classroom. By the time I was in the building my worrying was such that my vision was darkening and closing in, and I could barely see my way to the right room. Or I would get to class on time, then dream my way out of it, until, called on, I'd rush back from wherever I'd been, most likely just the other side of the window.

At that time every Hunter girl was required to take two years of Latin over the seventh, eighth, and ninth grades. We were taught Latin very slowly—the first year being divided into two—and this gave me a foundation in grammar and let me discover the satisfaction of seeing how sentences are put together, the words following rules that I could name and understand. I loved the precision of the grammar, the way the past perfect tense expressed an action before the past of the narrative and the subjunctive articulated undefined possibilities. In such a language time could be pinned down as well as place.

My teacher was Irving Kizner, short, portly, with a comic nose. For the first year of Latin his classroom looked east over Lexington, and in the morning the room was often flooded with so much sunshine that Mr. Kizner had to pull down the enormous shades. Even without the new darkness, there was a dreamy quality to the class. He was a born teacher, and his class was one of the few occasions during the school day when I wasn't distracted. Until his class, my life at school had consisted of one hurdle to be jumped after another. Now, when I didn't know the answer to a question, he helped me find it. When I knew the answer, it was exciting, not for the grades I earned but for the understanding, which felt like a steady place to stand.

Our Latin textbook was full of stories about *puellae*, using the verb *esse* in multiple ways. Often after the daily grammar and vocabulary quiz, after our stumbling translations of the simple text, Mr. Kizner told us a new chapter in his continuing tale about a GI who was lost in the middle of Italy during World War II. The soldier was a New Yorker, a native of the Bronx (Mr. Kizner lived in the Bronx and took the Lexington Avenue subway to school; I sometimes saw him on it). The soldier was separated from his unit and wandered in the Italian countryside until he took shelter in a cave and found an old woman. She was incalculably old, a Sibyl. Possibly, she was the Sibyl of Cumae, he suggested, drawing the Italian boot on the blackboard. Neither soldier nor Sibyl spoke modern Italian, and she no English. The only way they could converse was in Latin, which the soldier had studied in high school and college. The soldier's story took on a life for me apart from the pleasure of understanding what he and the Sibyl were saying in their simple Latin. The soldier was alone in a strange country, unable to speak the language; he wandered into a dark place and there found someone he could understand and who could not only understand him but also protect him by seeing the future. My whole life seemed like a riddle then—past, present, and future—but I felt that the answer was there, waiting to be heard, if only I could understand the language. Maybe I would wander into a cave, perhaps one of the tunnels in Central Park, and meet a Sibyl who would tell me what would become of me.

❧

Once my mother died I developed the idea that I couldn't remember things.

In school, it was crucial to be able to memorize and recite from memory, to know vocabulary, declensions, conjugations. I was supposed to know dates as well, of European history and American, and to memorize poetry from Chaucer to e. e. cummings. I did memorize in the word subjects—history, Latin, and English—but my capacity to retain what I'd memorized was small. The clarity of history as it rolled from date to date, battle to battle, legislative act to legislative act, began to melt and mist over immediately after the exam, until all that was left was the notion that there was a path to trace.

I gave up the idea of memorizing or retaining anything in mathematics or science. I could remember and apply the simple geometric formulae I was taught, but chemistry defeated me; algebra and physics drove me to tears. By eleventh grade, mathematics was over forever. Aside from a term of college botany in which I earned a D and spent hours in the greenhouse transplanting seedlings, science was over also. The mist descended and never lifted. I don't understand much of what happens in the world, from rain to the atomic bomb.

At bottom, there was something wrong beyond memory or the lack of it.

Though I could manage to believe that in 1776 the American Revolution began, I couldn't believe in atoms, chemicals, cells. Belief in what couldn't be seen seemed to me as much a question of faith in science as in religion, and God's mysteriousness was more visible daily than the rules of science.

A cloud of forgetting and a freezing of memory set in after my mother's death and came to seem a natural part of my existence. I thought that I was flawed, that my brain was damaged and the part called memory was missing. Memory is experience. I was busy not experiencing so I had few memories. Those I kept remind me of the silver baby cup that a friend's grandmother smuggled out of Russia sewn in the hem of her long bulky skirt. Dented, bent, the cup was all that had been salvaged, taken as a hostage from one life to another.

∽

The summer after I started Hunter, Valerie was away at camp, and I was sent off to relatives in Florida, later to join my mother and Sarah at my cousin's wedding in Atlanta. I went alone on the plane to Florida to visit with my grandparents, my uncles and their families. Maybe my parents thought it was time for a different kind of summer, although I don't remember wanting one or asking for a difference.

In Florida, I swam with Grandpa at his cabaña at one of the big Miami Beach hotels. I went to the family clothing store, Furmly's, on Lincoln Road, and visited my uncle and his family in a new bare development in Coral Gables where the trees and lawns had just been planted.

I saw my grandmother only a few times and I don't recall ever seeing her outside her small apartment, which was dark and filled with furniture and pictures, as if a whole house had been squeezed into three rooms. Grandpa and the rest of the Florida relatives referred to Grandma as one does to an invalid of known and fixed habits. I don't know if she left the apartment very often. When I learned, years later, of her daughter's death and the crushing depression afterward, my impressions of her made new sense.

She sat at a small Formica-topped table, facing the wall. The table was crowded with decks of cards, salt and pepper shakers, paper napkins, mail, bills, magazines, boxed sets of greeting cards, and a ball-point pen. It looked as though she lived at the table. Since I'd learned to write I had been sending her thank you notes for the five dollar bills she sent for my birthday in cards signed with her careful old signature. I expected to feel more for her because she was my grandmother.

I knew Grandpa from the visits he made when he came east on buying trips.

Grandpa had become diabetic, and on one visit decided that I liked ice cream too much. He had me choose my favorite flavor in the general store in Long Valley, and sat by me at our square oak kitchen table while I ate a whole pint. I'd lied and chosen Coffee. I ate the pint and didn't feel sick of ice cream. I tried to avoid annoying him when I was in Florida.

My grandmother smiled at me and asked how my parents were, but after each brief visit, I left the dark apartment, hustled out by my grandfather, relieved and guilty to be back in the blazing Florida light.

I stayed with my other uncle and his family in Miami Beach. Mornings, when my uncle went to work and the others scattered elsewhere, I was often left alone in the stucco, tile-roofed Spanish Colonial house. We'd never had a pet except for Valerie's parakeet, and my cousins had a little kitten in their backyard. I read all the time, sometimes emerging to try to make it to the hammock where I read some more. The kitten waited, often in a shed halfway across the yard, and waylaid me, jumping on my leg and clinging as if I were a tree. This branch of Furmans was hearty and oblivious, and I was ashamed of admitting that the kitten was bothering me.

Some mornings when I was alone, I'd walk away from the house a block or two, but I was timid about exploring. The sun was brilliant, the first Southern sun I'd ever felt. The light bounced off the white stucco walls and made them declare that there was nothing to see that wasn't already visible. The sun left dark shadows, and the coolness of the house when I returned was solace. I felt like an invalid or a prisoner at the end of a short chain. Adults know how to fill in time, and I began practicing in Miami, measuring how long it took to walk slowly up two blocks and back, watching the clock to see how many hours until my grandfather picked me up to go swimming at the hotel. At home, where my mother was within calling or running distance, time wasn't my enemy but a natural boundary, like the rising and setting of the sun.

One day my mother came to Florida with Sarah, and the next day we flew to Atlanta for the wedding.

When we walked down the steep steps from the plane, Aunt Sophie was there to greet us. My contact with Sophie had been through her annual birthday present from Rich's Department Store that came wrapped in a style different from New York stores, lighter, more ribbons, signs of another world. Sophie embraced my mother and cried. I hadn't seen a grown-up cry other than in the movies, and I was amazed that there was a person I didn't know, who was so attached to my mother that she'd cry at the sight of her.

I'd seen my mother with my Aunt Molly, who lived in the Bronx with her husband, a pharmacist. Molly helped him out at his store during the day when my cousins were in school. Aunt Molly was always in a hurry, a worry on her face, a gesture to us to move out of her way, her emergency was coming. While we cousins played in one room, they stayed in the kitchen and the sisters talked, Molly's jabbing narratives of incidents, Minnie's laughing and humming sounds of comfort, saying, *Don't take it to heart.*

Aunt Sophie both looked like my mother and my Aunt Molly and didn't. Her features were sharper than my mother's, her eyes smaller than Molly's. Aunt Molly's face was longer and narrower than my mother's, but when the three women were together they were unmistakably sisters. It confused me to have to place my mother with her family in an unknown past. The sight of my mother with Sophie—a warm, protective, bossy woman at the height of her powers, directing her only daughter's wedding—made me see my mother as younger and more fragile, more like me. For the first time I realized that she was someone with a life all her own, about which I knew nothing.

We stayed in the bungalow where Sophie and her husband lived, in the same house where my mother had lived with her mother, two brothers and two sisters, and her father until he was hospitalized permanently. You entered directly into the living room, went straight into the dining room, then the kitchen, all in a line. To the right of the living room was a hallway and off it a few bedrooms and the bathroom. The place was packed with people for the wedding, and a skinny old woman was stationed in the hallway at an ironing board for the whole week, pressing and starching clothes until they could walk by themselves. There were wedding gifts on every table and chair and piece of furniture. Fancy clothes for the rehearsal dinner and the wedding hung from lamps, and on the backs of every door crinolines floated like birds on water.

The wedding was held in an Atlanta country club (a Jewish one), that looked like something out of a Million Dollar Movie. The club had white columns at its entrance, and a pool where we swam a few afternoons. The inside was large and decorated in a color scheme of pale green, pink, peach, and creams, whose gracious symbolism was foreign to me. Compared to New York, Atlanta was practically wilderness: flowers and trees everywhere, people living in wooden houses, driving around in private cars instead of taking busses and subways. I had never seen anything like the country club before. Though it was not the richest or most elaborate club in the world, there was a prosperity and frivolity about it that was foreign to me.

Atlanta seemed in the advance guard, the real America, and New York something from the previous era of immigrants making a start.

Inside the club, I stood and waited for the wedding photographer to snap the pictures I was in so I could hide, knowing that I looked hideous in the dropped-waist blue-net dress with the velvet bow crossing my flat chest. Sarah buried her face in my mother's side. The sisters and brothers looked handsome and healthy in their finery, and it is pure projection to see them on the brink of the illnesses that felled them.

I've wondered if my mother was prescient, if she took the trip to Georgia for the first time since her mother's death because she suspected that she was dying. It's worse to think of her unwitting and innocent. In any event, she was blooming. In the wedding photos, my mother is animated and happy. I think she went to the wedding because of richness, of which her motherhood was a large part: three healthy daughters, one of them grown up enough to spend the summer away and the middle one soon off to camp for the second half of the summer; the five-year-old into the easier years. What's more, she was planning to work part-time for her old boss from the home for Jewish boys where she'd met my father. That summer was a turning point in her life. It was a time when the steady schedule of her life was about to change, and her trip to Georgia may have been her way of commemoration.

∾

When we got back from Georgia, I left home again and spent August at Buck's Rock Work Camp in New Milford, Connecticut. There were sports at the camp but also folk music, an orchestra and chorus (we sang parts of the Mozart *Requiem*), art shop, ceramics, jewelry-making, woodworking, the print shop (where I spent most of my time), and an animal and vegetable

Minnie Furman, Atlanta, 1958

farm. My mother and I wrote letters to each other; I called home, but I was really on my own for the first time. I never made the connection between the camp and my parents—that is, that they found it for me and chose to send me there. I returned from camp to country house, differently aware of the beauty of home but restless also, for the first time wriggling in my mother's embrace.

∾

My mother was admitted to Mount Sinai Hospital four times. One was for my younger sister's birth on May 9, 1953. The other three were for the illness that killed her. She went to see her G.P. in the fall when we came back from country. He might have been able to guess right away what was wrong and what would be the progress and the outcome.

She entered Mount Sinai Hospital on September 28, 1958. The hospital records state that she had a "three-month history of lower abdominal and back pain and increasing girth of abdomen." The exploratory laporotomy on October 2 revealed advanced ovarian cancer. Her ovaries had been "replaced by papillary adenocarcinoma baked into the pelvis." The cancer had already grown into the lining of her peritoneum (abdominal cavity), into her uterus, bladder, and bowels, and had colonized her omentum (the fold of tissue that connects the stomach to the pelvic organs and arteries) with a "hard firm stony mass thickened to about two inches in width and replaced by carcinoma completely to its insertion on the transverse colon." There were "numerous seedlings" on her liver but no large masses were found. She was released on October 16, 1958. She'd been in the hospital for nineteen days.

There was nothing to operate on, no possibility of excising the cancerous areas from the healthy. The cancer was a slow fire that was consuming her, transforming her internal organs to ruined nuggets. The wonder is that to chance living a little longer she chose to undergo a course of radiation, more fire, more transformation.

I don't know if she and my father ever acknowledged between them what was happening, or if they pretended, lying in their bed at night, that the prognosis was wrong and things would turn out all right, that their life together would resume, that she would start her part-time job, that the gardens and the house and apartment would be cared for, that we would grow and they would watch us leave home for our own adult lives. I don't think they believed that.

It is possible that the present business of daily life might have been enough for them: three children to be sent to school, clothed, and fed; an apartment to be kept clean and meals put on the table; a car that had to be moved from one side of the street to the other. The country house, the beloved house, now must have seemed like a large and distant burden. The business of being ill and functioning at all from day to day—getting dressed and trying to eat, taking the medicine, having the tests, having the radiation, absorbing new damage reports—this too might have been enough for her. The unbearable future was altogether unthinkable, for if she thought and he thought, would they have been able to go on?

When she died my father was left so completely bereft and alone and unprepared, I cannot believe that they made one plan for the comfort and continuation of the family.

How she could have believed that she would live, feeling as sick as she must have felt, I cannot imagine, especially given the fact that her mother had died of ovarian cancer fifteen years before. It is also possible, given the times, that she was not told of the sureness of her death.

I do not need to imagine the effort it took for all of us, children and parents, to pretend that she was not dying. My only hope while she was dying was to ignore what I saw, what I heard, and what I felt. In practicing obliviousness, I was trying for a miracle. I was trying to keep her alive, and my effort continued after her death until obliviousness became the norm and what I felt, heard, and knew was to be ignored at all costs. Twelve years after my mother's death I was on a tourist bus in Kenya, and the guide announced that the scene below us—the world severed—was the Great Rift Valley. It looked like a vast geographical picture of my small history.

∽

I began to menstruate. I don't recall the day or time or even the year, but my mother was still alive. Early on, my parents had given Valerie and me a book for children on sex and reproduction, maybe around the time my mother was pregnant with Sarah. I could read the words but I understood nothing. There was a photographic illustration of a much-magnified fertilized egg that might as well have been a blurry night sky.

I don't remember the physical sensations of cramping or even the moment of discovering the bleeding. I don't remember the onset of the feeling that I would keep until my menstruation ended: surprise, annoyance, and inadequacy. For decades I was never quite prepared for the regular monthly event. I took my father's advice to ignore what was annoying or unpleasant. I didn't make a conscious connection between ovulation and menstruation, that is, between my ovaries, the same organs which had betrayed my mother, and the expulsion of blood from the lining of my uterus.

Menstruating changed my dance lessons. I was self-conscious about wearing the pad and sure that I smelled, that everyone would know, though what difference it would make to anyone else in class—all women and girls—I didn't consider. Instead of making me feel like the others, menstruating made me feel different. The pad I wore to absorb the blood felt like a wound between my legs.

∾

She was out of the hospital, at home, from October 16 until March 27.

We went on a sloppy winter afternoon, late on a Sunday, to the Russian Tea Room, a lavishly grown-up restaurant, with slightly worn, lush decorations, tall vases of flowers, lots of mirrors, and banquettes which were awkward to sit on if you were smaller than full-size. I don't know what possessed them to take us there. It was an expensive choice for a family that never ate out, a celebration at a time when there seemed to be only bleakness and worry. It might have been Passover and my mother not up to cooking her last Seder. I worried that the other diners might notice my mother's condition, her tooth-pick arms and distended belly, how slowly she walked, even with my father's support. If it was meant to be a celebration in defiance of sickness and death, then they should have left us at home because it takes an adult consciousness to pretend pleasure. I wanted only the ordinary, the before. What I would have given anything for was a Seder with my mother's roast chicken, her matzoh balls in strong chicken broth.

My mother ordered Chicken Kiev, a boned chicken breast rolled around a stick of butter, breaded and sautéed until the outside is crisp, the meat soft, and the butter melted. Under pressure from my mother's knife the chicken breast popped open and butter spurted out like blood from an artery. At the end of the meal, the Chicken Kiev was still on her plate, the first cut still there, the butter a puddle. Her abdomen was distended because it was filled with fluid. If she ever felt hungry, it must have been an impossible desire to fulfill.

❧

I did what I was asked to do—I visited her in the hospital, I accompanied her shrunken body to the radiologist and helped her home—but I was not a good daughter. I had always been her favorite, and now I was looking beyond her.

Her illness made her a burden. For the first time I had obligations to her as well as the simple love I still bear. I had to accompany her in a taxi, sometimes two busses, to Fifth Avenue across from the Metropolitan for her radiation treatments. The door to the doctor's office was on the street, and we invariably opened it to a crowded room where we waited unconscionable amounts of time. We were never late. My mother was frail and leaned on my arm. I didn't want to be there. I didn't know how to talk to the receptionist for her or how to care for her. I wanted to get on with my life, my new school, my new independence. It annoyed me that the radiologist was on the East Side, just like Hunter. I wanted that trip across town to be mine alone.

I believed that you went to a doctor for medicine and to get better. She had never been sick. It was my father who was allergic to nuts and bee stings, had rashes on his skin, hay fever in the fall. I knew what bothered my father, but I didn't know what she required besides her eyeglasses for driving. Not only was she healthy, she was strong and tough. I wonder if she took pride in her sturdiness, pleasure in her capacity for work, her competence at housekeeping and gardening, and if part of her pride meant not going to the doctor when her abdomen swelled and her back hurt. For years it was my secret anxiety that she might have saved herself had she gone for help sooner.

I learned much later that ovarian cancer can't be detected by normal gynecological exam, until it is essentially too late. Put off seeing the doctor for a busy summer when your niece is getting married and the oldest girl is off at camp, the middle one in Florida with her grandparents. Put it off. You're forty-six and that's nearly middle-aged. You're putting on weight, rounding out in the belly. The pains you feel, the pressure on your stomach, middle-aged indigestion perhaps. There are too many things to do to go into the city to see the doctor—white-wash the living room, care for your five-year-old, get ready to travel to the wedding.

My mother didn't have a chance.

For years I assumed it was my father's decision not to tell us that she was dying, consistent with his reluctance to talk about anything troublesome. When I asked him about it late in his life, he said that she wanted it that way because she would not admit that she was dying. She knew how serious her condition was and still chose the hopeless ordeal of radiation in order to prolong her life.

Whether she did this to please him or spare him, to spare us or herself, I'll never know. There is no one left to ask.

❧

Hunter required that we wear for gym a bright blue cotton gym suit and white canvas sneakers. Since my sneakers didn't stay white for long, I used white shoe polish on them. The smell of the chemical mix and the drip of the white liquid from the fabric ball at the end of the twisted wire, the hiss of the hot iron on a still-wet gym suit: I never remembered in time that gym was the next day. Often I ironed the dirty one so the steam rose, bearing sweat. Often the shoes didn't dry and I had to carry them to school in a paper bag, still smelling lethal. It was the beginning of a lifetime of feeling unprepared. I needed money for lunch and carfare, and I needed an allowance. Now I had to get everything from Daddy who didn't know enough of my routine to anticipate my needs or remind me of them, and I was inadequate to the simplest demands of my daily life.

Though my mother was leaving us inch by inch, no one came out and said so, neither she nor my father, none of us children. I'm not sure that even if I had been told I would have heard. We ignored death at our peril and lost each other. From being my best refuge and support, my mother had come to demand my company, and I suspect that she was as bewildered by the change as I, though maybe not. My mother had the benefit of her own experience. She went through her own adolescence in a household where a terrifying disease was present. Perhaps she understood what I couldn't. Her own mother had died of ovarian cancer, a fact she knew though I wouldn't until much later, so perhaps she was well aware of what was happening to her. Even though she was far from Georgia during her mother's illness, she and Sophie kept up a regular correspondence, so she would have learned the progress of the disease. Perhaps she was stunned by what was happening to her body and we all receded into the background. We were the noisy living, the train pulling out of the station without her.

∽

After school I walked past the Russian Embassy on Sixty-eighth and Park, past the luncheonette where I sometimes went for a toasted buttered English muffin when I had the money or could borrow some, and I took the Fifth Avenue bus uptown to the hospital to see my mother.

The entrance was on Fifth Avenue. There was a dark blue canopy, then four steps up to the lobby. This time she was in a semi-private room, and the other bed was empty. Her bed was the one close to the window, and the trees across Fifth Avenue in Central Park were just visible, the top of the trees and the blue sky of the April day.

Aunt Molly was sitting in an armless chair between the window and the bed. She held her purse in her lap, her hands on the top of her purse as if she had just come or were about to leave.

I put my pile of schoolbooks on the foot of Mommy's bed, and Molly frowned. I didn't see where else to put them. Mommy's bedside table was covered with glasses and a thermos, a box of tissues, and the phone. The little cabinet by the wall had Molly's coat over it.

My mother asked about school. It was okay, I told her. I had the feeling that I'd interrupted their conversation. Maybe that's why Molly frowned and not because I'd been too casual with the hospital bed, with my mother's fragile legs.

They had quarreled recently enough to need a talk. Maybe they were making up, once and for all, for the insult Molly felt the spring before when Mommy hadn't included my younger cousin in Sarah's birthday party. Molly looked sad now, more sad than angry, but still angry.

I told them school was fine. I liked Latin, and my English teacher was great, and we were reading Beowulf: *Grimly I grappled my grief to my bosom* . . .

"Be careful where you step," Aunt Molly warned.

"Be careful," said Mommy, and she turned her head so that I looked on the floor where there was a small puddle of vomit and blood.

"No one's come to clean it up," Aunt Molly said. "I went down the hall to ask."

My mother reached out for me and I went closer to her, slowly making my way down the bed to her arms, skinny as the arms of survivors in liberated camps, but her face was not blank like theirs. She longed for me. She wanted me close. I reached her and leaned over the bed. I touched my lips to her dry cheekbone. The sheets smelled of sweat and a funny sweetness not from perfume but from her body.

I wanted to get out of there but when I was down on the street, running to the crosstown bus stop, I knew there was nowhere else to be.

∽

I can't escape from the fact that my mother didn't tell me she was dying.

It would have made all the difference. It would have spared me from everything. Her death would never have moved to the realm of the unsaid and the mystical, the destined. It would have stayed in the more ordinary realm of biology.

According to one close friend of hers, my mother didn't know "she had cancer until quite late—complaining of intestinal problems."

Another friend wrote:

At that time, there was a conspiracy of kindness—anyhow, it was thought to be kindness—to keep the patient from finding out the truth. Maybe that made it harder for the patient; I know it made it harder for friends. Instead of talking about serious decisions, you had to sit there giving false comfort. Was your mother frightened? Yes, of course. She was a clever woman; she knew what drastic treatment she was getting, and she was frightened that she wasn't being told the truth—maybe in their hearts people like that always know if they aren't being told the truth. But when there's a crisis, a terrible one, the thing to do is follow the conventions of the time. And the conventions at the time your mother got sick dictated cheeriness, encouragement, fake hope.

Everything that happens in a family is a result of the emotional whole. My mother could no more have acknowledged her illness and prepared us for her death and absence openly than she could have avoided her doom. It was the family way, to forget and to dissemble. My father never explained my mother's disease to us. My mother never told her friends that she was going to die, though maybe to her there would have been no solace to be gained from that. After my mother's death, I began to say, *Oh, I can't remember a thing about my childhood.* It must have seemed that if I were to go on living without her, I would have to leave even memory behind.

She returned to the hospital March 27 and left April Fool's Day. She was home for about three weeks, and readmitted on April 24. She died twenty days later on May 14.

∽

A year after her death we returned to Mount Zion Cemetery. A stone had been put up at Mommy's grave.

My father had chosen granite from Barre, Vermont. On top of the stone was chiseled WIFE, on the slanting front her name, Beloved Mother, and her dates: August 10, 1912 and May 14, 1959.

In his sketch of the stone Mr. Fier of Riverside Studios Inc./Monuments abbreviated August, and my father wrote to him that he wished it spelled out and also: "To bring the two dates together, as you specified, both date-lines should be reduced to $1\frac{3}{8}$ inches high. Each of the date-lines should be centered, and need not line up with each other right and left. Thus, the name will have first prominence, Beloved Mother second, and both date-lines third."

∽

I was riding the Lexington Avenue bus home from school. I was thirteen and a half, birthday in November, and the month was May. It wasn't winter anymore but it wasn't yet warm. The bus was crowded with other Hunter girls, and as the bus pulled away from the gray stone castle, someone said that my sister had been looking for me all over school. We usually avoided each other, so this was an occurrence so unusual that even if there hadn't been plenty going on to alert me, that should have. I considered going back to look for her, but it was too late, the bus was moving, and I was glad to have eluded her.

On the bus I knew that someone dear to me was gone. The atmosphere of the crowded bus, the noise of everyone talking all at once, the strangers who looked at us, annoyed at our commotion, our shouting messages across their heads, squeezing them and crowding—I heard it all and was there, yet everything was also put away from me. The feeling that someone dear to me was gone was so intense that I leaned over and mentioned it to a friend who had managed to find a seat. She didn't reply, and I felt the first futility of sharing such a sensation. I was diminished. My life was changed. The noise and the movement of the bus were happening to someone else who was living as if the dear person were still there.

A friend, the son of a colleague of my father's, was leaving New York. The family was moving to Baltimore. Pierre must be the one who was gone. I thought it odd to have such a strong feeling about this boy when even I had to admit to myself that what I really liked was the idea of him, a boy I could visit, one who lived around the corner, a boy in my life. He had invited me several times that winter to his dancing school. He went to a private school and the lessons might have been *de rigeur* for him and his classmates. They were an agony for me. I didn't know how to do the dances: waltz, box step, polka. I was always wearing the wrong thing, didn't have the right white gloves, and my mother, who was too ill to go shopping or even to notice much about my dress, mightn't have known about such things in any case.

When I reached home, my father and sister were in the living room. My father had a drink in front of him on the coffee table. The glass had in it two cubes of ice and whiskey splashed over them. The glass was wide at the top, like a person with arms raised to the sky. My father was sitting on the couch, hunched forward. Valerie sat beside him. When I came into the room, she signaled me not to ask questions and took me to her room. Valerie lit a Marlboro, shocking me because she was forbidden to smoke. She told me that Mommy was dead. She offered me the cigarette, shocking me again, and I smoked it. Mommy had died in Mount Sinai Hospital. She had been consumed. Frail, skinny, down to bone, all the words that say and don't say what I knew somewhere in my heart it meant: No one looks that way and lives. Mommy was dead. I tried to cry, thinking I should cry. I thought of Daddy alone in the living room. We went back to him but he didn't volunteer any words about her death. He didn't say if he was with her, if she was conscious when it came.

Sarah was downstairs at a neighbor's apartment, a family with two little girls with whom she played often. Now it seems inconceivable to me but I believe—because she's said so and Valerie too—that Sarah was not at the funeral and that she wasn't told until after the funeral that our mother was dead. What did anyone imagine the child would think was going on? She'd had her sixth birthday five days before. She'd notice the change in routine, the change in our faces, the phone calls, the flowers, the food in the house. By her exclusion from the shock, the grief, the chaos, even to the muted degree my father and older sister and I allowed it to be experienced, the harm landed on her most roughly.

⁓

I wish I had been there when my mother died. I wish I had been there when she died to hold her hand, to see her out, and to weep for her; also to believe that she was dead. I wish I had been there when she died so that I could have said Goodbye and believed that she was gone forever.

I used to be able to stop at the top of a *jété* and hover the way birds do in flight. I jumped over puddles and crevices in the earth, confident that I would get to the other side. To remember the time between my mother's first hospitalization and her death, I have to trust that I'll get to the other side.

∽

It is one thing to be sorry not to have been with my mother at the moment of her death, but what about the 198 days between October and May? I've lost those days forever and all the feelings. I spent all my time and energy running away from home and her, and now would give anything to have been there.

∽

The funeral was held where my father's would also be thirty-three years later, at Riverside Chapel on Amsterdam Avenue. Afterwards, for as long as I lived in the neighborhood, I avoided walking past it, and even turned my eyes away when I rolled by in a cab or bus.

I didn't go up to the coffin until it was almost too late, and then didn't have the courage to touch her or even to look at her face. I recall a shoulder in a lined box.

We went to the cemetery in a limousine, to the city of the dead, the limousine knowing where it was going, tracing through the neighborhoods and family villages of graves to the Furman plot. The sun shone brilliantly on the green lawn where there was a place dug for my mother's coffin. The rabbi, whom I didn't know, said words. My father stood by the grave. We stood next to him. On the way out of the cemetery, I rushed ahead and tried to take his hand. I wanted to comfort him. I thought it would make a pretty picture. He pulled his hand away and preceded me to the limousine.

Lots of people came to our apartment, more than had ever been there before. My parents had never had a city party, only occasional friends for dinner. Who prepared the food and drink? Late in the afternoon I was telling a story, describing my eccentric summer camp to the circle of friends. How exhilarated I felt to be entertaining them and how loudly they laughed. It was probably laughter of relief that they could forget why they were there or laughter of indulgence or pity for me, or relief that no one else had to speak while I was holding forth. In a lull my father said, "My friends. I never thought I would say this, but I have to ask you to go." He was exhausted, he said. He needed to be alone. I felt ashamed for performing. I felt the performer's panic when the audience leaves. I had miscalculated the moment and striven to show off in a way I might have if my mother were alive instead of in a coffin in the family plot, where we'd newly left her. It still seemed to me that she would come home.

∾

I began to think constantly about my future, not only what would happen to me but when I would die. *How* was not in question. I knew that I would die of ovarian cancer, and I knew as surely what it would feel like to be told that I had ovarian cancer. It would feel like the last piece of a jigsaw puzzle being pushed into place.

∾

With my mother's death the old rivalry between Valerie and me subsided to occasional skirmishes, and Sarah and I stopped squabbling, stopped saying much of anything. I removed myself from them, physically at least. Nothing would ever be the same again. My father came into focus as he hadn't been when she was alive. The only parent now, he was too important to us, also too much of a wreck from grief and surprise and from the burden of us to do us much good day to day. Valerie tried to assume an authority that no one but death had granted her. Sarah was more inaccessible than ever, clinging to Valerie.

∽

Did Mommy make fried chicken? I wrote to Valerie thirty-seven years later.

Not that she recalled but every maid did who came to take Mommy's place. *Fried chicken,* she replied, *plates of it in the refrigerator. Probably because it was a dish that they could leave and get home.*

∽

In my mother's place at the kitchen table when I came home each day was a large black woman with a shining necklace of a scar that reached from one side of her jaw to the other. She didn't like us very much, and I became aware for the first time of the need to be liked in order to get food and clean clothes. No act of love or kindness, given or received, has ever seemed automatic to me again.

∽

One night about a year after my mother's death, my father told me that Bill Stern had died in a sailing accident. Madeline had called to invite me to visit, and my father made the arrangements for me to take the bus over the river again.

I had thought death unique to my mother but now Bill had been taken also, and even more swiftly. In my touchiness and grief for my mother, I dreaded my first glimpse of Madeline as I believed others must have dreaded seeing me. She was thinner, and darker somehow, but glad to see me. The baby was beginning to walk.

After dinner I read Lucy a story and stayed with her until she fell asleep, not because she needed me to but because I wasn't sure why I was there or what I should be doing.

In the big kitchen, Madeline was heating milk and honey, and she used an old white enamel saucepan I recognized. She said that Bill had gone for a quick sail before they were due over at a neighbor's for dinner. I wanted her to talk all night about how she'd heard he was dead, when she told the children or were they there when she was told, and, most of all, how she was sustaining herself. Madeline didn't say much, though, and I didn't ask her any questions. I was unable to talk about my mother and the taboo spread to Bill.

The next day we went to a nearby lake. I stayed on the grassy shore, watching the children while Madeline swam with a slow, methodical stroke to a white raft that was anchored some distance out. She returned and watched the baby while Lucy and I swam.

Halfway to the raft, the girl said, "I can't touch bottom, can you?"

"No," I said, "but you can swim, can't you?"

I looked back to shore and Madeline waved. She flapped the baby's hand in a wave to us.

"Oh, yes. I can swim." The little girl smiled, her wide mouth stretching.

She tucked into the water and disappeared.

I looked down in the water for Lucy. Madeline and the baby were playing with a ball, rolling it back and forth between them. I dove down into the water, lost my breath, and cried out, filling my mouth with water. It was cold and dark beneath the surface. Bill and my mother waited there. I couldn't find the little girl, though I reached my arms out for her and turned around and around. I gasped and reached for the surface, dove down again, tried to find her, rose again, and saw her a few feet from me, smiling. She swam over and put her arms around my neck. When she let go, we began making our way back to the shore.

◦~◦

My second summer at camp I felt my difference from the other campers. I felt like an embodiment of the saying, *She's growing like a weed.* I grew taller, skinnier, developed small breasts I hunched my shoulders to hide. I grew untended and unobserved until I grew to be ashamed that my mother had sickened and died. Her illness seemed to be my fault, not a fault of an action on my part but of my being. I might have appeared to carry my difference as a sign of superiority, for one waspish girl said, "Oh, stop feeling so sorry for yourself about your mother." It seemed shameful that I had let my misery show, and perhaps one reason that I have remembered her remark all these years—and forgotten kindness and affectionate words—is that its cruelty spurred me to divert, to dissemble, and in that way to stop feeling.

I was better off at Buck's Rock than I would have been anywhere else.

Since I had been there the summer before, I considered it part of my past life. Being away from my parents and sisters had felt like a clear look across a valley to my adult life which was promising and unknown. At Buck's Rock for the second time, I experienced a sensation like the darkening of light. I had always had the capacity for pure, even overwhelming, feelings of joy. Lying on the hump of our lawn and staring up at the clouds, I sometimes imagined my destiny but more often was able simply to breathe in the delicious cold smell of the grass and transport myself onto the ledges and steps in the clouds. Now when

I felt the surge of such pure happiness—unconnected to past or future—I caught myself and truncated the sensation. I had forgotten something. What was it? A promise? An appointment? Something I was supposed to do? I had forgotten myself. I had forgotten my mother. I had forgotten that my mother was dead. I had dared, I had relaxed. I was bad and therefore would always slip in that simple, egotistical way and forget. It was a confirmation of Valerie's opinion of me, often expressed: egotistical, irresponsible. Long past that first summer, the shameful realization of having forgotten and having done harm by forgetting, took on a life of its own and became a familiar sensation that substituted for mourning.

Out of my constant turns of emotion came the conviction that now my adult life had begun, and I was meeting people—the lover or husband, the friends—I would have forever. I believed that I was setting up patterns for a busy, tragic, turbulent life that would leave me something like Marlene Dietrich at the end of my life, alone in a dimly lit room, a cigarette and a drink my only company. I savored and feared such an image of myself, curious and excited to know the end, as if my life were a book I couldn't read quickly enough.

That summer kissing began, full of saliva and juicy lips. I learned about kissing, and rolling about on blankets on the forest floor, crushing leaves and pine cones, being stabbed by sticks. I was not really aware of the physiology of the boys I kissed and was kissed by, and though I grew excited did not know where this might lead. My head was full of lore from song lyrics about going too far and fast girls, but this didn't connect with what was going on in my body or in the smooth-skinned male bodies I tumbled with.

I didn't want to talk about my mother's death because if I spoke of her death, it would have meant a contamination of one life by another: my present in which I was sealed off and pretending my mother hadn't existed, the past when I had been surrounded by my mother's presence. No one informed me about the hereditary possibility of ovarian cancer (if it was even known then), but the bond I felt with my mother linked me with her disease. I had changed in my body, unobserved by her, and I'd become a young woman. Still, I carried her inside me, located specifically in my abdomen. Scientific drawings of the female reproductive system showed me only what other women looked like. Inside my abdomen waited patient black space that would be the end of me.

In the last days of August when our projects were coming to an end, camp looked like a stage set. School would begin soon, and I would be alone once again.

∽

For the first time I felt like an expensive child. My father mentioned before I left for camp that he was feeling strapped, and he talked about the cost of my mother's illness and the funeral. Anxiety about money became a constant theme for my father, the one outlet he permitted himself for complaints that he was burdened singularly with our family life. He must have had the anxiety all his life; it was part of his character. He educated us, he helped us out until he died and left an inheritance for each of us, but he never completely lost his anxiety about money. Decades after my mother's death, I believed that he was still paying off her funeral, was still burdened by the cost of her illness. Before my mother died I knew we didn't have a lot of money. After she died I felt that we were on the brink. In fact, we had already fallen off, though not financially.

My father's incompetence set in right away. He had seemed like an extremely capable man: intelligent, well educated, talented, hardworking. But my mother's ability with the world masked both his reluctance to engage with it and his deep desire to be left alone. After she died, he became even less interested than before, more harassed and burdened, until each small repair or household chore became an extreme annoyance and interruption.

Sometime after her death we needed sheets. This is a memory like an old coin, images flattened and obscured over time. We had one double bed in the apartment, two single beds, and in Valerie's room a large hassock that unfolded into a bed. Our sheets were washed at the Chinese laundry whose windows were clogged green by a maze of stringy plants thriving on the steamy air. The sheets came home to us clean, pressed, folded, and wrapped in crisp paper. In the country the sheets were washed in the machine in the kitchen and dried outside on the line. Now, all our sheets for all the beds tore simultaneously, another leak in the household balloon.

It is a sign of his desperation that my father sent me to Macy's with his charge card and a list of bed sizes.

After school I traveled downtown to Thirty-fourth Street on the Lexington Avenue bus and walked across town to Herald Square. B. Altman's was open then, and I passed Ohrbach's along the way. I'd been to Macy's before, but I didn't know where a person bought sheets. I summoned up courage and found someone to ask. I went to the proper floor and there found more mysteries. The linen department was a vast expanse of tables, Klein's-like, each with a sign identifying a category I didn't understand. I didn't know what muslin was or thread counts, and I couldn't ask. The muslin sheets were cheaper. For the first time in my life I understood that whatever I decided to do would be the wrong thing. I didn't just feel as if I were doomed to fail, I felt that there was no other choice than to fail, in the absence of information, in the absence of my mother. I didn't excuse myself. I knew that I was useless to my father. I bought the sheets and got them home. Did I go back to exchange muslin for percale, did my father or Valerie? I gave him back the charge card and went about my selfish business.

❧

We got a beagle puppy after my mother's death, and we named him Dostoevsky, sometimes calling him Dusty. Valerie and Sarah adored the dog. No one was exactly responsible for him, and at night the dog stayed in the kitchen with the doors closed and the floor covered with newspapers, sometimes wet and sometimes soiled. No one was exactly responsible for picking up the newspapers.

Neither did anyone want to walk the dog, and we argued two, three times a day over whose turn it was. My father was at work by day and at night he was often out, busy with a new social life of dates and dinners. Sarah couldn't go down to the street alone. Valerie liked to be in her bedroom, smoking cigarettes, watching TV, talking on the phone to her friends. She preferred the dog to me, she often told me, but badgered me into walking him. I didn't like to walk him to the park past the brownstones, once family houses, now broken into apartments and crammed with Puerto Ricans, new immigrants, raucous and comfortable on the street as I was not. It embarrassed me to walk Dusty, to watch him sniffing excitedly, and when he peed, especially when he defecated, I wanted to get away quickly. This was in the fall of 1959, when I was fourteen.

One evening after I had walked Dostoevsky up and down the block, I pulled him as usual to the door of our building. A man followed me in and waited with me for the elevator.

Usually there was a round, white-haired doorman sitting in a carved throne in the big lobby, uncomfortable and poky, sighing his shift away, but he was not there, only I, the dog, and the very tall man who had followed me in from the street.

He went in the elevator after me, and when I pressed the

button for our floor, he chose a higher floor. The door closed and the elevator began to rise. He grabbed me and tugged at my underpants, saying, "Let's see what you got under there." Somehow he got his pants open and revealed a huge erection. In the small elevator, the dog yapping, the man so tall and the hallucinatory erection—I didn't know what it was—I screamed, and I pounded the elevator buttons and the alarm button. The elevator reached a floor and stopped, ever so slowly, sinking a little, rising to a stop, the door creaking open, and I pulled away from him and dragged the dog out after me. I pounded on an apartment door and pressed the bell, calling for help. The man ran past me, down the marble stairs. An old woman stuck out her head and demanded to know what the noise was for.

"Ignore it and it will go away," my father said. "Nothing happened, did it?"

I answered the phone in my parents' bedroom, now my father's alone. A boy spoke. I didn't catch his name. He asked if I ever stuck my finger up my crack. He said I knew who he was. I didn't know who he was and I didn't know what he meant by my crack. I listened. He must have been dialing randomly and by his good luck found me, docile, compliant, too polite to hang up. When I finally did, I felt guilty.

Ignore it and it will go away: my father's dictum. *Nothing actually happened,* he said, about the man in the elevator, the boy's phone call. I hadn't been raped. But since I knew only vaguely about sexual matters, it seemed to me that my father was saying that the disturbing words hadn't been said to me, and the pull on the elastic band of my underpants hadn't happened, the strange hand hadn't touched me. There was no one there to say, *Nothing happened to your father but something happened to you.*

❧

Valerie says that Daddy gave her pieces of Mommy's jewelry but I believe she stole them because that's what I did: a tiny enamel pin inlaid with green and blue flowers, a choker of fake Baroque pearls of gold, silver, and white. Over the years, I visited my mother's jewelry box for proof that my mother had existed. For his own quiet reasons, my father kept the box in his top dresser drawer until he died.

Other than the box and the portrait of her that my father had painted in 1939, there was nothing in the city after her death—aside from us, her three daughters—to say that my mother had ever been there.

The unchanging, cyclical nature of country life was kinder to her. Her jars of preserves and pickles rested on the shelves by the kitchen door. The rooms didn't change as they had when she was alive and improving the house. For the year or two in which we continued to go to the country, our life remained connected to her. In the country I began my long wait for her return.

❧

We went to the country less often. Valerie had long since refused to come with us, preferring to stay in the city alone, and a weekend with Sarah and me in the house must have been melancholy for my father.

Through the Hunter literary magazine, I'd become friends with Kathryn, who lived in a three-story, plain-fronted red-brick house in Greenwich Village. We both wanted to be writers. We took walks to the bottom of Manhattan Island from our school, and often ended up at her house. She made an art of nervousness, hands shaking, drinking coffee devotedly. She could recount her childhood in excruciating detail, as if it were a country she was exiled from forever. A family trip across country in a station wagon with wooden sides was a novel she intended to write. In a letter written one summer, Kathryn named the "Problem of Places," like that, with capital letters, and rattled off six evocative images, a "shell path in Cape Cod...." She said that wherever she was she wanted to be elsewhere, creating a small problem of the disloyalty of memory, the advisability and impossibility of cutting off yearnings that memory creates, then capping it by asking if it wasn't wrong to seal minds up.

Her father was a character out of J. M. Barrie, temperamental and explosive, and Kathryn's gentle mother was always home and always cooking something. Once in a while when she had to empty out her ancient crowded refrigerator, before their Christmas party or Thanksgiving when she needed room for new food, out came old baby food and jelly jars filled with mold and unidentifiable lumps that she would puzzle over before dumping. In their dining room, next to the long harvest table, was the unabridged dictionary they used to settle family word-fights at meals, most often between Kathryn's father and brother. There were older sisters—one a classmate of Valerie's at Hunter—but the brother had the glamor. He also wanted to be a writer, and I thought he had the better chance because he was a man. It was a word family, and I didn't know enough to wonder what the feelings were beneath the words. I was always glad to be there rather than home, and to try to fit into any family but my own.

One weekend in early spring my father drove me, my younger sister, and Kathryn to the country for the weekend. We left New York, as we always had, on Friday night and drove into the dark evening. Winter was gone, the ground was no longer muddy, but the nights even in the city were chilly.

Kathryn and I were in the back seat, and Sarah, soon asleep, up front. It made everything new to have Kathryn along on the ride, and I worried that nothing would be good enough for her—our car, the food my father somehow provided, though not the house or the country; these I had faith in even without my mother. My family had always sung on the drive to the country—lullabies, show tunes, and Gilbert and Sullivan. Now Kathryn and I began to sing "Sometimes I Feel like a Motherless Child," all the sad verses, "Sometimes I feel like I'm almost gone, A long way from home." I was carried away by the sound of our voices, worrying that mine wasn't as sweet as hers or as musical, by the dark night outside the car window, the strange places we'd never stopped and wouldn't. My father asked us to sing a different song. It was a moment like the one after Mommy's funeral when Daddy asked all the guests to go home. Too late, the song, the persistence of our singing its many dirge-like choruses, seemed a terrible affront to my father. The phrases I think of to capture my shame are clichés of manners and behavior—better left unsaid, not for company—a world away from a mourning so all-encompassing that I didn't know it was there.

"Sing something else," he said. "Or stop singing for a while."

The house felt abandoned, as always when we arrived, but the next day the sun dispelled the oddness of my mother's absence. We were young enough that the country, the buzz of the insect and bird worlds in spring and, for me, the novelty of having Kathryn there, substituted for care.

The next night when it was dark and supper was over, Kathryn and I took a walk in the moonlight to the Flockstown schoolhouse. To be out at night with my friend, to walk away from the house into the darkness, with the sound of the wind through the trees nearly tangible, made me think that I had reached adult life at last, though the ticket of entry was my mother's death and absence. If she were alive and in the yellow-windowed house, I might not be walking with Kathryn up the well-known dirt road in the dark, walking to the crossroads at the top of the hill and following the path through the sticky winter weeds and the first greens of spring to the steps of the old wooden schoolhouse.

There was hardly a speck of paint on the outside of that building, though on the clapboards protected by the porch roof there was a white, powdery coating. It had been that long since anyone had tried to preserve it. We didn't go inside, maybe because we were too scared or the night was too grand to leave.

We settled on the steps singing again, one of the sweet-sad folksongs that we thought we'd invented, like our wrap-around skirts and clunky sandals. The scrubby daytime weeds and the road beyond were white in the moonlight. A figure was in back of us, at the corner of the building. In the white quiet the night birds stopped peeping. The figure was in front of us. I saw it dimly and it was gone.

We decided it was the ghost of Shakespeare. It was a benevolent ghost, much less frightening than my mother's ghost would have been. It was a kind of handing over, that moment: here was a way out of the apartment in the city and the house in the country where nothing was the same, away from my father who wanted to be left alone, from my sisters who were a team that excluded me, and most of all away from myself. I wouldn't be my mother's flesh and blood child anymore. I'd be a word-thing. I'd make everything into a story, and change myself from "I" to "she".

❧

Now here was a sight. On a patio over a cruel-looking New England river, two women of fifty or so sat and talked. Once in a while, light rain fell, dampening our clothes, but we didn't choose to go inside the tiny restaurant. We hadn't seen each other since neither of us knew when. Beth was as familiar to me as she had been when we were children, and yet a stranger. We told each other our husbands' names, the ages and names of our children. Her children were old enough to be my child's parents. You haven't changed, she told me. Neither had she, I said.

"You know," she said, "when your father was planning to marry Netty, he introduced her to my parents. She told my mother, 'I'm marrying Sylvan, not his daughters. I have no intention of being their mother.' My mother was shocked, of course. She told me, and I was shocked too."

The passing confidence had been given thirty-four years before. Her mother was dead, and my father had died recently. Triumphant, ashamed of my childishness, I clutched this news from the past. Proof at last, but what was I to do with it?

"What could your father have been thinking of?" she asked. "What was your stepmother thinking of, marrying a man with an eight-year-old daughter, a sixteen-year-old, one just going to college? A woman in the mother's place with no intention of being a mother?"

My father was thinking of himself, I answered. That's what most people do.

He was thinking of what he got: an end to his mourning; the fierce love, unswerving commitment, and constant companionship of an attractive woman of compatible interests until death parted them; his late middle years and old age not alone; a new life.

In a way they were daring. If they'd been characters in a book I might have admired them and wished that the scowling storm of an adolescent stepdaughter would take the hint and go away.

Sylvan Furman

Sometime in the second year after my mother's death, Anna Mae Smith came to work for us. She brought us stability. The house was clean once again, the laundry done, folded, and ironed; dinner was something to look forward to, and she stayed late to serve it and to do the dishes on nights when my father was out at meetings or on dates. Anna Mae had a long ride north to her own apartment in Harlem and it was clear even to me in my fog that she had people to care for who were her own. She stayed with us so long that it began to seem as if she had known my mother, though she never had, as if her providing for us was the last remnant of my mother's presence.

Before my father remarried, I wrote a short story. My hero's name was Frank, and he was stolid, almost speechless, since I didn't know how he felt about anything. I wrote about his troubles, which I don't recall, and which he solved by shooting himself in the head. I had shot a gun only a few times, a rifle at target practice at camp, but I could think of no other way either to end the story or to make things right for Frank. I showed the story to my father. He read it standing up in the kitchen. "Very nice," he said, "but not quite ready for publication."

I was not so different at base from the majority of adolescents. I had never been especially patient. I hadn't had the chance to develop a belief in things working out more or less and more often than not. What was in the present seemed to be what would always be. For my unvoiced missing of my mother, as constant as my love had been, there was no help. I began to want more than anything that things should change, because the present, though compelling, was not bearable.

❧

I was familiar with the idea of a stepmother from the fairy tales that scared me as a child. Hansel and Gretel, Cinderella, Snow White: the stepmother takes the place of the mother, then tries to get rid of the children. Literature had prepared me for a dramatic struggle but not for the entirely different drama that would take place, more layered and subtle, and far more compromising to me. My compliant nature, my desire for a mother, urged me toward my stepmother, who was funny, lovely to look at, and worldly in ways my mother wasn't. It didn't occur to me to try to see from her point of view why Netty at forty-nine would marry a man of nearly fifty with three daughters, nor did a possible variant to Grimm: The mother dies and the stepmother has a daughter of her own to care for and three stepdaughters to clear off, and there are at least six dramas occurring and in five I figure as a walk-on or small speaking part at best.

❧

She's pretty. Where did you find her, Daddy?

This is what my stepmother remembers my saying when we were introduced, an occasion she places at Buck's Rock in a diner where the campers went for ice cream after swimming and where visiting parents traditionally took campers for a Saturday lunch out.

I don't remember saying what Netty recalled, although I have a hazy recollection of sitting in the diner with them, excited to be away from camp, wondering what to order to eat. My cute question is plausible in its desire to please my father.

When I met her Jeanette Cohen was a stylish woman, small and prematurely white-haired with sparkling eyes and a resemblance to Joan Fontaine. She dressed in outfits, sweater sets and below-the-knee straight skirts, suits with a scarf flung around her neck, and even when she was casual in the country her clothes were coordinated. She looked like what she was, a professional woman, and she said often and proudly that she'd worked since college, taking time off only briefly during the war to follow her doctor-husband around the United States with her infant daughter. (Her daughter was a year younger than Valerie, two years older than I.) Netty had worked most of her daughter's childhood. After Netty's divorce, her widowed mother had come to live with Netty and her daughter Nancy, and her presence made Netty's self-sufficiency possible. When Netty was five, her father died in the Spanish Influenza Epidemic of 1918. Like all the deaths of that epidemic, his was unexpected and swift. Her mother managed, with her own mother's help, to keep their house in Jamaica, Queens, and to raise Netty and her brother.

I never thought of Netty as another child of loss, and I never learned why she and her first husband divorced. When she spoke of him it was to relate an anecdote from their romance or the war. The vital figures in her life were her mother, her women friends, and her daughter.

She had graduated from Barnard, sister school to my father's alma mater, Columbia, and had known since college some of our Larchmont and New Rochelle friends. Though my stepmother was certainly Jewish—on one side English Jews who had moved to Jamaica, West Indies, and on the other German Jews—she was more American to me than Jewish, a career woman, and my mother whom I'd never seen go to temple or do anything more Jewish than cook matzoh ball soup and blintzes, seemed by contrast a peasant immigrant.

The dichotomy between my dead mother and my live stepmother seemed natural and unquestionable—the only easy fit around. My mother's background came to seem deprived, lower class, at a disadvantage compared to Netty's, though hers too had its difficulties and central tragedy. The real disadvantage my mother suffered was of course death. There was no question of a rivalry between a dead woman and a live one, except to me.

As for my father, he was besotted with her, in love in every way and also, I suspect, relieved that he would not be alone with us anymore. Her daughter had just graduated from high school and was going to the University of Wisconsin, as was Valerie after an initial year at Hunter College. Perhaps now Valerie felt free to go, leaving Sarah in the hands of a stepmother. It was her time to go, in any case. The deal Daddy and Netty worked out at their merger might have gone something like this: Valerie is gone to college and need be home only on holidays. Laura is almost sixteen and has two more years with us. Nancy is unused to having sisters so little will be asked of her. Sarah is eight so she is with us for the longest. Sarah will be her father's responsibility alone, and if this means she doesn't have winter boots—she doesn't know how to get them for herself and no one anticipates or sees her needs—then so be it. She will get in time what she asks for—music lessons, music camp, eventually boarding school. The Furman girls are their father's; Nancy is her mother's; no pretense at family, but a civilized sharing of space. Financial responsibility for the Furman girls is Sylvan's. Responsibility for the household is split: separate checking accounts in this marriage and Netty does the shopping for food and household goods and the managing of the household help. Netty would not pretend to replace our mother. Our mother would not be a part of the household.

❧

I place my first meeting with Netty at Passover, but perhaps she is right and we first met at Buck's Rock. In any case, by Passover the relationship was set: they would be married in

August. Who chose their wedding date I don't know. They were busy, employed, parents—perhaps they both took out their date books and landed on a day that lay equidistant between Valerie's birthday and my mother's because it fit into their work and vacation schedule, and when Sarah and I would be away. If my father noticed the coincidence, he never made mention of it to me. I noticed and promptly forgot the exact day of my mother's birthday and Valerie's.

Netty brought a friend along to our Seder. Netty's manner was laughing and a little brittle as my father led the service. She was demanding to be admired, most of all wanting constant response. With her friend she was more relaxed, and her jokey questions, the apparatus of her conversation, were relaxed and confident. She was at her best with her friends; with them she needed neither to prove her loyalty and affection nor to assert her claim to theirs. She trusted her friends, as she didn't trust us.

The friend was amused by Netty's antics but—perhaps I am imagining this—a little worried by them as she glanced at us and at Daddy, checking our reactions.

"Why is this night different from all other nights?" Sarah recited, as we'd coached her to do. Netty was intent on proving her difference from us that night. If she had been to a Seder before I can't be sure, though in the decades that followed of Seders with her and Daddy, Seders at their apartment, there was never such a fuss from her again about the oddness of the Passover customs. It is hard to explain her need to put herself forward that night. She might have been nervous that on that night, different from all other nights, my father's memory of his wife might be strong. It is such a time-marker, the Passover, a holiday of such temporal portent that it's possible to wind a year around it and to say, Mommy died not very long after Passover. A year: it seems that soon that Netty appeared at our

Seder table, but it was two years. It might have been twenty and felt the same.

Laughter, humor, jokiness, wit: the stories I told about camp after my mother's funeral, Netty's intercutting of our talk with jokes, funny questions, a turn of our phrasing meant to make us laugh; humor became the outward sign of inner disloyalty perhaps because laughing is so involuntary, so pleasurable and so hard to stop. I wonder if anyone else would have found Netty so funny. A large part of her humor was her painting of herself as a naive iconoclast, her wide-eyed knocking down of idols and institutions, religious, academic, political—except for Barnard and Columbia and certain powerful left-liberals and their causes.

I might have learned from her joking not to be intimidated by the world I was growing up into, but instead I understood evidence of Netty's superiority. *She* wouldn't be cowed by authority; *she* wouldn't be stopped by some officious person from the phone company, the school, the post office, or the bank. If I wanted to wake before anyone else and go to religious school and then a brief service at temple, a shrug, a wink, a laugh. She had another mode of righteous anger: Grocery-store managers were raw meat to her and salesclerks who failed to deliver to her, the Customer. She was just as swift to praise someone who was helpful and she wrote letters—which she quoted to us from memory—to the person's supervisor. This letter of praise would go into the employee's file, she informed us. She was an employment expert and knew that such letters could help the person's position in the company, which I believed, though I doubted that a complaint had equal negative power. This was a far cry from the days of my mother when I was afraid to return something to a store, afraid to ask for help from a clerk. I clung to the old ways, and came to loathe Netty's accounts of her triumphs in the field where I, determined to stay my mother's child, failed.

What did she find so hilarious that night? The table that was set with the best cloth and napkins, my grandmother's silver plate, the white china with the gold band? That wasn't funny but splendid to my eyes, impressive enough for her, I hoped, for I must have instinctively doubted my father's ability to protect me any better than the absent fathers of Cinderella and Snow White. Was it the questions, the Four painfully memorized Questions? The platter Anna Mae had prepared under my father's hurried guidance, the matzoh folded in the ironed white damask napkin? On the platter was our version of a roasted shank of lamb, a roasted chicken neck. The charoses looked as always like chopped apple and red wine—no nuts because my father was allergic—and a boiled egg is a boiled egg as parsley is parsley with a small bowl for dipping forevermore. The dipping bowl of salt water, tears for the slaves of olden days, was green, one of a set my mother and father commissioned from an old man in the Pisgah Forest when they drove down to visit my mother's family in Atlanta. Maybe the ritual started Netty off, the dipping, the tasting, the remembering and my father's recital in Hebrew and English of his abbreviated version of the Seder. "Those are very interesting and intelligent questions you asked," he said that night to the Four Questions as he always had.

The essence of the Passover ceremony is the egg and the platter on which it rests. The sprigs of parsley, the shallow dish of salt water, the horseradish root, the stand-in lamb shank, the peeled boiled egg, the matzoh itself—and I would include the white tablecloth and the gold-banded white dishes, the grandmother's silver plate—all are symbols of the renewal of the season, the start of the spring, the end of the school year in sight and the summer ahead, summer as it used to be in the country, summer as it was at camp: all are symbols and portents of that which would come to be, one portent after another of the next thing.

Netty sat back against a layer of pillows, her attendant nearby and watchful. On Passover we took the throw pillows from the couch or even our bed pillows in fresh cases, and reclined as the ceremony required, but she was sitting against her pillows like a pasha, and she joked. Everything was funny to her and every new Hebrew utterance from my father, each new word and phrase that told the story of Jewish slavery and Jewish deliverance a new cause for laughter. He laughed too. Maybe she wasn't sitting on one of the couch pillows at all but on her laughter, like a cartoon character rising on clouds of smoke. She wasn't just laughing at God and the Jewish people. She was laughing at my mother and our family, at me as I watched.

There was a lesson to be gained from that Passover: she was to be the center of attention. My father was to be part of her, their marriage an endurance race that would be won by them.

∾

There were two kinds of phone calls at Buck's Rock: one through the office, when you were paged over the loudspeaker or another camper came running to the place you were known to be, in my case the print shop; the second and more common, the call to the phone booth outside the dining hall, the call that came during supper. The first was more formal, never chatty, for information to be passed along. The second was for talk: news from home, news from camp.

One August evening I got a call during supper. It was Daddy. He and Netty were married. They were on their way to Jamaica for their honeymoon and were calling to say goodbye. Ceremonially, he handed the phone to Netty, and she and I spoke. Though it might not have been the very first time this order of movement took place, it became set: he initiated the call, he and I spoke briefly, and then the phone was handed over to Netty. At our very worst times, this came to seem like the coin I had to pay to be allowed to talk to him. Very late in his life when I was living far away, he used to phone—sometimes at night, sometimes during the day, always when Netty was out. I had the feeling that our calls—desultory, swapping our little news—were illicit and had to conclude quickly. Our calls never ended without my feeling that I'd left something unsaid, cut him off before he was about to tell me the real reason why he'd wanted to speak to me. That evening in 1961, however, he was in no position to tell me to be polite to her, to be nice; she was probably within earshot. And even if she'd been across the river, he would not have asked in so many words. He counted on attention to his wishes, to anticipation of his wishes and then compliance with them. My mother had taken such care of him and we were expected to also.

The call couldn't have been my first inkling that they were going to be married, but in memory that's the case. Other campers took the train into New York for orthodontist appointments. Surely I could have been summoned to be included in their wedding. Even Sarah, who had been sent to Atlanta to spend the summer with Aunt Sophie, could have been included. If they thought of it and discounted the idea as too much trouble or our presence too much of an imposition on their moment, I'll never know. *Bon voyage.* I went back inside the noisy dining hall. They were on their way whether I liked it or not. It had nothing to do with me.

Later that summer I was again summoned to the phone during supper for a call, this time from Valerie, Daddy, and Netty, all three telling me with much laughing and joking a long and complicated story that had to do with a rainstorm, a hurricane, and the dog, trying to get to the airport from Schooley's Mountain, trying to get Daddy to a plane for Miami. Valerie was complaining that she had no clothes and was in shorts and a halter top, soaked to the skin and freezing. Netty was relating a story, graciously, about some forgetting of money or ticket that she had rescued my father from, she, the little woman, the brains in the outfit. The reason for all this hilarity, for their comedy of mishaps and good intentions? My grandfather had died.

∾

We couldn't stay in the same place. Netty's apartment on West End and One Hundred and Sixth—a place I saw once, when it was packed up—wasn't big enough for the new configuration, and neither was ours. While I was at camp, Daddy and Netty had searched for an apartment and found one on West End Avenue. For years I'd been entering my friends' apartment buildings on West End and Riverside Drive (which felt in winter like a trip to the country). Now we would be on West End Avenue, though the entrance to the building was on the side street.

My mother's portrait came off the wall and wasn't hung again for decades, not until my father gave it to me out of the blue. Anna Mae took Dostoevsky home with her, and though I vaguely promised I'd visit, I never saw him again. I returned from camp to boxes, and a stripped apartment. If memory is experience, then I never moved from Ninety-fifth Street. Someone must have packed and sorted, gotten rid of the last ragtag bits of my mother's possessions, our outgrown clothes, toys, books, kitchen goods and tools. Some of our furniture or dishes or glasses were moved to the country and only the dressiest or most useful pieces taken to West End Avenue, but I don't know who made the decisions. Our dining-room table was folded permanently and stood forever in the foyer, holding mail, keys, and a lamp. The little pine chest where we put our ice skates, mittens, and hats went into a corner under a mirror also bought long ago at an auction.

The apartment we moved into was dark much of the time, hidden under the slanting shadow of the building across West End Avenue. The statue of Joan of Arc on horseback down the gloomy hill on Riverside Drive was the nearest ornament. Years later, after my father's death, Netty mentioned that when they were looking, they'd hoped for a view: the view from the living room on Ninety-fifth Street was a good one, a "city view," straight down the island. And she'd had a wonderful river view on One Hundred and Sixth Street. They'd taken the one they had because it was available. (All along I thought they'd taken it because they liked it.) I felt praised personally that Netty had a good word for our old apartment and that she told me about their search. It seemed like such an adult confidence.

Ninety-fifth Street, like my mother, was not bid farewell. Netty spoke mournfully of her apartment, recalling her years there, her old mother, her time as a mother, but we Furmans didn't say anything about our past.

Nancy, off at college, got a big bedroom in the new arrangement with two beds and the furniture from her original room. My older sister slept in the dining room when she was home from college, and she was rousted out in the morning by Netty to let Anna Mae clean. Sarah and I didn't have to share a room anymore. Her bedroom was large and on the same side of the apartment as Nancy's and our parents' bedroom. I got the maid's room, off the butler's pantry, a dark small room overlooking the backs of the surrounding buildings, with a toilet of its own and a sink in the room. There was a bathtub in the toilet room, a deep square basin that no adult or child over the age of seven could have stretched out in, and none ever did in my time. Soon it was filled with boxes and used for storage.

Netty and Daddy went out often—to the opera, the ballet, the movies, the theatre—beginning the happy marriage that continued until he died. They had good friends and once in a while gave dinner parties. The country house in New Jersey became anathema and we didn't go very often. It didn't suit Netty to go there. Why should it have?

I was afraid of displeasing Daddy and Netty, though I didn't know how to please them except through compliance and trying to amuse them. If my real identity were to be seen—my mother's favorite, the child I'd been all my life—then I might lose this home also.

No one told us not to talk about our mother or the past—our whole lives, really. My father's wish that all should go smoothly and his pain when it didn't was instruction enough. My mother, by making things go so well, had trained me to want to take care of him; in this case, caring for him meant obliterating her. She had been dead for two years. It was as if she'd never existed. If she hadn't existed, I didn't either.

❧

I didn't always go to a friend's house after school nor did I linger away from home on long walks until dark. Often when I didn't have something to do at school or a friend to be with, I went to Bloomingdale's, blocks down Lexington Avenue from Hunter. It was a staid store then, with a cloakroom for ladies' furs and packages, and merchandise not so different from B. Altman's.

To start, I wandered on the ground floor. The handbags and costume jewelry looked grotesque. I preferred antique jewelry of which I had none or tiny stud earrings bought in the Village store where I'd had my ears pierced. I went to the mezzanine and walked by the bolts of fabric, taking the cut ends between my fingers, reading the labels as if I were considering, though I didn't know how to sew. The Cosmetics department was right below the mezzanine, and I walked along the shining glass counters, studying the bottles and jars of creams and colorings, hoping to learn what they were and what I should use. Around this time I began to wear an Elizabeth Arden cream rouge in a rose tint that had no relation to my own color but was too pale to be noticeable.

I knew where all the departments were and visited each by elevator or escalator, which I preferred because it was less claustrophobic, but the basement was the place I really shopped, among the moderate-priced clothing and the bargains, clothing that had been marked down in its original department, marked down again and maybe again, until it took its last stand here. There were racks and tables of clothes, the sizes often jumbled and mixed so that I could search for hours, waiting for the right thing to present itself to me. It was a treasure hunt, one I was so absorbed in that when I looked up and scanned the walls for a clock, I found that I had to leave. Only when I was out on the street, retracing my steps up Lexington to school so that I could still use my bus pass home or—if I had any money—taking the bus across town from Bloomingdale's, only then did I wonder that I had let so much time slip by. My dreamy hunt seemed odd to me, but if shopping had been a drug to inhale or swallow or inject, it would have been no less irresistible. I bought piece upon piece of clothing that didn't fit and that I wouldn't need unless I changed identity.

Sometimes I had my father's Bloomingdale's card with me, but more often when I found something I wanted, a saleswoman had to call my father at work, and he would give permission for the purchase. Up to a certain amount, ten dollars, I was allowed to charge without permission, but sometimes, unknown to me, he would arrange with the credit department to put new restrictions on the account. I'm not sure if I wasted a great deal of my father's money or if my spending anything at all set him off. If my mother had been alive she would have been shopping with me and we might have quarreled about the items I wanted. As it was, the purchase either of a blouse that I would never wear or a necessary winter coat were equally suspect to my father. I didn't learn to discriminate between the necessary and the extravagant. Both were equally shameful to me, first from the tension of the call to my father at work, the interruption and possible refusal, and later the necessity of facing him at home.

I was usually starving after school and never seemed to have enough money to get all that I wanted to eat, but by the time I got home a greater hunger was on my mind. Then Anna Mae was the hurdle, to greet her and get past her as she sat in the darkening kitchen with the newspaper before her, and to ignore what I noticed of her loneliness and boredom, even her affection for me, and to go into the maid's room, put down my schoolbooks, arrange my Latin homework on the desk, then lie on the bed and fall asleep. I have never known a deeper sleep. As soon as I lay down on the bed and closed my eyes I fell into a black pit. Maybe I felt safe with Anna Mae so near, turning the pages of her *Daily News*, a rustle I heard only once before I slept. The falling down was a pleasure. The dreams I had were haunting as a headache.

In the blackness I was free, but awakened I was in the family: the sounds of Daddy and Netty home from their offices, the door opening, the keys dropping on the hall table, picking up the mail, their calls, his "I'm home," Netty's "Woo-hoo," if she were in a good mood. Greeting Anna Mae and asking where I was—my shut door a sign that I was in my room—and then their footsteps across the linoleum and the carpet, fading from hearing, across the apartment to their bedroom. Anna Mae would bustle then, filling the ice bucket, re-warming or finishing dinner, and soon I heard my parents having drinks in the living room. I rose from that wonderful sleep in which I was released from body and mind, to resume my performance as a daughter and stepdaughter, as a guest in their house, to join them and try to think of something to tell them, to get through the family night.

∾

I still have afternoons that are identical in feeling to those afternoons after my mother's death, after my father remarried, when I would do anything to stay away from home until it was dinnertime or dark, when I began shopping as a way of losing time.

Or I walked, took a subway or bus in some direction for the slimmest purpose, then walked all the way home up and across Manhattan Island.

Or I would go home straight from school and fall onto my bed, only to awaken when Sarah or my father or Anna Mae called me to dinner and I would drag myself up from a round dark well and join the new family for dinner. Tinkling bell. Dinner is served.

When I remember the origin of these wandering afternoons, I turn my car toward home and hope that when I get there I can sleep it off. After all these years, the mood asserts itself as the single truth: Here I am again, it says, I've never really gone, just hiding and biding.

There's a name for the mood, one that sums up and dismisses the entrapment and the suffering, and sometimes if I say the word soon enough, the word I dislike and shirk, I may escape the condition: Depression. If I say clinically depressed, I feel even better.

In the new apartment, mornings were no problem. Everyone was in an equal rush to dress and get out of there. Though I often cut it close, I was rarely late for school. How Sarah made it out I don't know. Logically I can reconstruct a scenario of Daddy urging her to wake up—she was always a slow riser—to get dressed, get to school, but I can't hear the sounds or see him or Sarah. They were on the other side of the apartment and as far as I was concerned might have been in Kazakhstan.

Each classroom at school was a separate world, and I was a different person in each regrouping of classmates, in gym and Latin, English and history. I never felt like a full member of the group of friends most important to me. They were a year ahead of me, and I always thought of the difference as if we were marching through life in assigned places and they would get there first.

Along with Kathryn, there was Noreen, a pale, lovely Irish girl from Brooklyn, a little awkward and dreamy; Lizzie, a quick dark Jew from Park Avenue, funny and not quite sure why I was there; and Sonya, who lived on West End Avenue south of our apartment, whose home seemed secure and whole. I felt invisible enough there to be comfortable.

There had been trouble in Sonya's family: her father was dead, her mother the sole support of Sonya, her older sister Helen, and brother. On several tables were studio photographs of the dead father; the shape of his head, his intelligent and melancholy expression were echoed in his children. They were Russian Jews, displaced and international, and yet the girls—I knew the brother very little—were confidently American as well. They'd been raised speaking English, Russian, and French. Helen was not quite as shiny as Sonya but she was kinder and serene. As a child, Helen had been maimed by radiation treatments on her ankle and she limped, but she made the lumpy scar and her rolling gait seem unproblematic. I envied Sonya her friendship with Helen, with whom she shared a bedroom, and with her mother who ran the house with authority. She was a tall, sturdy woman with long blonde hair that she braided and pinned into a bun. She had a round French boyfriend who was often there, who brought flowers to her and was courtly, even flirtatious, to her daughters and their friends. I had a role to play around him of innocent young girl. Indeed, I truly was innocent and ignorant, though my mother's death made me the bearer of knowledge that I believed none of my friends possessed.

Sometimes all six of us did homework after school in Sonya and Helen's room, schoolbooks and notebooks spread out in our little spaces. I didn't do much actual work. There was silence and the mutter of irregular verbs being memorized or a math problem solved with much erasing and re-inscribing, then someone would say something and the heads would lift one by one and we'd talk.

Or this is a picture culled from memory and *Little Women*.

Evening came. One girl peeled off for Brooklyn, another for downtown; one started her walk east across the park, and I stalled, hoping for the dinner invitation which often came. I cringe now at my hopefulness and silent waiting. I did even then, but I was willing to be humiliated to avoid going home. I wonder if I'm exaggerating or if it's true that they often invited me to be able to start their own dinner. Even if they didn't think of me deeply, perhaps they guessed that there was something I was avoiding for I didn't invite friends over to my house. Or perhaps they had the egotism of family and accepted without question that I preferred their home to mine.

Once the invitation was made and I accepted, I phoned home. If Netty answered, she was irritated because she'd in-

Laura Furman, age nineteen

cluded me in her meal-planning and here was a last-minute change. My father hesitated. I dreaded his saying, though he didn't, *Haven't you been eating there too often?* Or, *Let me speak with Sonya's mother, please.* It was a lucky sign when Anna Mae answered and told me they weren't home yet. I announced that I wouldn't be home, felt a tremble when she said, "All right, honey. You have fun." She was weary and bored, nothing to do with my appearance or absence, spending the late afternoons at the kitchen table, turning over the pages of her paper like a prisoner. I felt I'd let her down by not being there.

After dinner I knew enough to leave promptly, or so I hoped. The darkness as I walked the nine blocks north on West End Avenue was broken by spotlights and the lighted canopies of the grander buildings. The streets were deserted, and I often started to run at Eighty-seventh Street, dashing into the lobby of my parents' building, panting. In the darkness I had to admit that I was alone, and that terrified me more than the street dangers. It astonished me to arrive at the quiet apartment, my father and Netty in their room, Sarah in hers, sometimes a voice calling out, "You home?" and to realize that all the time I had been out there, they were in here and hadn't known—hadn't thought of—where I was and what I was doing. The apartment felt safe but suffocating, and I flattered myself that I belonged outside in the adventurous dark.

If I came back extra late, I was sometimes met by a sight out of a story that I hadn't yet read. My father sat in the dark, on Netty's yellow sofa, a drink in front of him. He was in the same place if I awoke and came out of my room in the middle of the night, sensing someone else awake. Once I asked him why he sat there in the dark, and he asked me if I'd read a very good story by a man named Jerome Weidman, "My Father Sits in the Dark." Jerome Weidman had worked for Grandpa long ago when the Furmans were still in Brooklyn, and Grandpa bragged reproachfully to my father what a good son Jerome Weidman was to *his* mother.

Sitting in the dark as he was, my father greeted me as if I were something pleasing he'd just remembered. A new marriage, his children, the still recent death of my mother, a job he might have found more tedious than rewarding: he had plenty to think about in the dark. I waited for reproaches for missing dinner or being so often away or for being later than I'd promised, but I didn't get them. I greeted him and slipped into my room. If I stayed and talked, I felt as though I were keeping him from something, but when I made my good-nights I worried I was leaving too soon.

If I got home and Daddy and Netty were still awake, there were other hazards. I went to say good night, not entering their bedroom, their embarrassing privacy, but stayed in the doorway, able to see only my father's legs as he lay in his bed reading. Netty was in her bed and she would talk, as if I were a daughter come home, as if the stories she told me were something I wanted to hear. I was trapped in the doorway; she might have been trapped in her bed. I had a newly developed horror of being rude and I didn't know how to say good night, neither to my second mother whom I hardly knew, nor to my father.

∾

It would have been better if I'd stayed in my room until dinner. They would have been happier alone, telling each other about the day at work, but I felt obliged to sit with them and listen to them talk about things I knew nothing about, and try to find something about my day that they might like to hear. I ate peanuts, careful not to eat too many, and looked at the cartoons in *The New Yorker*, their voices and laughter louder the more they drank.

Drinks ended at six-thirty on the dot when Anna Mae appeared and said that dinner was ready. Netty opened the doors to the dining room and we filed in—someone going for Sarah who stayed in her room during drinks—and took our places at the table. Anna Mae rolled in the food on a three-level cart, and set the covered dishes on the table or on the sideboard. We'd pass our plates to Netty and she'd serve us the vegetables and the starch. Daddy carved the meat and put the portions on the plates passed to him. Toward the end of each meal, I began to get impatient, knowing that Anna Mae was waiting in the kitchen for us to finish so that she could do the dishes and go home. A few times when I made cowardly half-suggestions and offers to do the clearing up, Netty made clear that this was the way it would be. Netty paid for Anna Mae's Social Security, a valuable contribution, which seemed all too abstract for me. All I felt was embarrassment at keeping Anna Mae waiting.

No matter how much I ate, I left the table hungry. Netty knew how to stretch food: from Sunday roast to stew to bony soup, and, though her planning was admirable, her economy took the pleasure out of the food for me. The stretching came from her natural economy and her genuine pleasure, even glee, in controlling the destiny of every scrap of food that came into the house. She labeled food in the refrigerator—this was for Sylvan or Netty—so that no one would eat a special cheese or treat, or leftovers meant for another meal.

The only time I felt comfortable with my father was when he and I were reading my Latin homework, Cicero, Caesar, Vergil, and his Cassell's dictionary our happiest links. My father's desk was in one corner of the dining room, and in another the single bed where Valerie slept when she was home from college. By the window overlooking West End Avenue was a bookshelf my father had built for the Ninety-fifth Street apartment. In a cabinet underneath, our photos from the life before were stored. I knew they were there but I never looked at them, as if they were forbidden. On the wall opposite my seat, was my father's oil painting of Dick Morgenstern's big white barn.

At dinner one night, Netty announced that she had completed her plan that day for what she wanted done with her body at her death. She had been in touch with the medical school at Columbia and ascertained that they would be very happy to have her body. None too soon, she told them, was her hope! If she died young enough for her eyes to be useful to someone else, well, that was fine. It was all up to them. Otherwise, a student would learn from the dissection, and she wouldn't be taking up space in a graveyard.

Daddy made a sound like "Tttctch." He had developed a gesture that became his most characteristic, positioning his hands as if he were pushing something away from himself and patting the air to make it smooth in front of him. It was a gesture asking for silence and distance, and this might have egged her on. Her husband's disapproval was a red flag that flushed her cheeks.

I sat on her right, facing the oil of Dick Morgenstern's barn. While she spoke, I rode in the back seat of our car while we drove slowly past the barn on the way to visit the Morgensterns. The girls were waiting for us to play. Faith and my mother would talk—on the terrace? All of the children would walk down the path that was bordered by prickly berry bushes to the little open-air room where there were benches we climbed on to reach the fattest berries, and we'd eat until our mothers called us in. It seemed very important to be able to remember exactly going past Dick Morgenstern's barn.

Netty turned to me. "It's a very good thing. A far better thing than a burial. What a waste."

She talked and her voice got so soft I could hardly hear her anymore. It was simple: she had forgotten who I was. She thought I was a dinner guest and she was entertaining me in her frank and honest way, talking as if my mother was not now in a graveyard taking up space. If I told her who I was, maybe she would stop.

My father said later, "She didn't mean anything by it." But after that night I believed that Netty's remarks were part of a campaign to obliterate my mother's existence in a way that her death and illness hadn't, not for love of us by any means, or even for her genuine and passionate love of my father, but from her love of self-expression, from an uncontrollable desire to say what she damn well pleased. Once she made up her mind, she gave no air or light to doubts. *What would be the use of that?* she might ask. *What's the use of doubting once you've made up your mind?*

❧

And yet I wonder. As time went along, once I was out of their apartment and on my own—and particularly since I married and became happier and more settled—she became someone to whom I have turned for advice. My stepmother has been in my life so long now that at times the vividness of my memory of how she was then seems both untruthful and impossible to deny. Since my father's death, every time I talk to my stepmother, brief conversations in which she is Granny to my son or calls me *my love*, wishing she could see me, see him, have us closer, I wonder if it could have been different, if I am missing something about her in that time. I apply my imagination to the task of reconciliation: she was a woman who had been independent for a long time, whose daughter was going off to college, a woman in love who could see the time when all of her love's children would be out of her way, and his. The wish was mother to the action: she would not be our mother, we would soon be gone. But we weren't. Her love is dead, his daughters remain; the youngest alienated, the eldest across an ocean, and

I a thousand and a half miles away, still trying to make a mother out of her. My own mother might have wished nothing more than for me to have a real second mother, but out of loyalty to her I didn't acknowledge even to myself for decades that I wanted a mother. *I had a mother,* I would say fiercely if anyone suggested that this or that might betoken a search for a mother.

I always end up saying: *But that was long ago and in another country, and anyway it's over,* and it is, until the next time I start figuring again, figuring and re-figuring how it might have been different if we had been different.

∞

During this period, my father didn't know what I was up to half the time or even where I was.

I rushed from one place to the next, and, wherever I was, worried about the next thing. If I caught myself relaxing, I'd remember: Yes, but where will you be in a year, a week, a day? When I cried, riding the bus and hiding my face, lying in my bed at night unable to recapture the deep afternoon sleeps, I knew that nothing awaited me, that no one was tracking me, that I didn't have to rush.

∞

Sonya's family gave parties for all generations, though the adults tended to stay in the dining room eating homemade delicacies and drinking wine while the young sang and played guitars in the living room. Her mother served small and delicious *piroshki*, with buttery, flaky dough, and meat ground to tiny pearls, more pastry-like than the doughy Polish dumplings I found later when I lived on the Lower East Side. Their parties were exuberant and inspired illusion: we were in Paris, not on West End Avenue, destiny was at hand. I met a prince whose family name I recognized when I read *War and Peace,* and

I stared at a golden-haired boy while he played Villa-Lobos on his guitar.

But there must have been intoxication other than the music. During one party in the early spring, I went into the bathroom and found a razor blade and made a cut across the middle finger of my left hand. Drops of blood fell into the old-fashioned square white sink. I watched the small puddle spread on the wet, crackled surface until the outer edges were brownish, a color far from the red center. Then I went about binding my small wound and I returned to the party.

There are two neat lines, parallel, scarred on that finger. I was not trying to kill myself, to begin to bleed to death with Sonya's mother's shower cap and drying stockings watching me blandly. I wanted someone to notice me: that is the simplest explanation I can construct at this distance, and it is probably the truth. It was too embarrassing to say then; it is even embarrassing now. While I was doing it, it seemed senseless yet expressive. I couldn't say why and I couldn't say what, but I didn't stop myself from doing it.

I walked home alone, my hand clutching the toilet paper that absorbed the little blood I produced.

It was Easter or nearly so. I wanted to die and I didn't at all. I wanted a cataclysm, I wanted time to stop. Six weeks before the third anniversary of my mother's death I was beginning to be convinced that she was not going to come back. I wanted to put a stop to the quiet, the not mentioning, the darkness pulled over her life and her motherhood, and the message not to remember.

News travels fast, my diary records. I was called into the guidance office at school and told to seek professional help.

I told my father that I was unhappy and that I had cut myself.

—*We all have problems, no, periods of…*

—*Oh, Christ, Daddy, this has been happening all year.*

My father was then executive director of a mental health association, and he chose for me a psychiatrist who was on the board.

The doctor's office was on Park Avenue, between school and Bloomingdale's. The entrance, and this pleased me, was not through the lobby, where I would have had to pass under the eyes of the doorman. It had a door of its own, and down three steps its own private waiting room, and was closer to the corner, to the side street that meant escape, although it must also have been accessible through the lobby because the doctor was paralyzed. He walked with crutches and his legs swung limp in his good wool trousers.

I awaited his help, for all the attention I had gained frightened me. I frightened myself. I had done something I didn't understand. *How much is plenty of this?* I asked the diary about both my sadness and my efforts to keep going to school in the face of it. I accused myself often of laziness because of sleeping in the afternoons, getting Bs and Cs in school, and not being happy. *How much cowardice? I can't pull myself up anymore. I just want to run and God knows where to. My hands shake, dr. says blood has infection, swollen glands. Command: sleep. I don't get tired. I am afraid to say it to myself. What is this—bankrupt at 16—there's more years aren't there? Cuts heal and go away, right? Whatever it is it has to stop. It's not even laziness anymore.* I was not seriously insomniac and I didn't hallucinate. I was desperately unhappy, and I had no idea why.

I expected that the first session would be the first of many. At the end of years with the shrink, as I called him in my diary, I would understand what was wrong with me. Trouble might pop up now and again, but I would know what to do about it. Someday I would emerge from his office in stockings and high heels, no longer wearing glasses, well dressed and grown up, my suitcase in my hand, hailing a taxi for Grand Central, leaving New York for an adult life.

At our first appointment, I sat opposite the doctor, his shiny dark wood desk between us, and I glanced surreptitiously at the couch and chair on the other side of the small room and up to the street level where people passed on innocent enviable errands. I told him about cutting myself at the party, about when I cried and could not stop. The doctor's voice crackled constantly, as though he needed to clear his throat one more time and a pure tone would emerge. The first session was on a Thursday and my father had told me that another was scheduled for Saturday morning. After only a little talk, however, the doctor had a surprise for me.

Ten minutes of me nervously talking and whammy....

He told me to go home and that my father would take me to Tower Nine of Roosevelt Hospital where I would stay for a while. I left his office. I walked straight down Lexington Avenue to Bloomingdale's and bought a nightgown and a robe for my hospital stay.

∽

I knew two people my age who were in mental hospitals. One boy stayed for a while at a private hospital on the Upper East Side. He had done nothing dramatic—not that he told me. He'd quarreled with his parents. The other, a girl I'd met at camp and who had cracked up in her first term at college, had been at that hospital and at others, and by the time I went to Roosevelt she was in a public yellow-brick hospital in Queens that looked like a factory. Though we didn't know it, she would spend ten years in and out of hospitals, trying more than once to kill herself, nearly succeeding a few times. She would lose her youth to hospitals and medications, a prisoner of the mysterious course she was on and of her mental patient's dossier.

Hospitalization, her despair, her suicide attempts, the regime of pills and shock treatments, her exile from her development and her peers, seemed to her to be the price she was paying, and now I was too, she told me, for being bright and sensitive. I was pleased to be called bright and sensitive by her, for I admired her, and hers was an explanation that delineated us and them, that held the key to my feeling that there was no right place for me.

What's more, my constant reading had familiarized me with the idea of the nervous breakdown, of people having more feeling or trouble than they could bear and being hospitalized as a result. I read *The Crack-Up* until the binding snapped and then I kept the book together with a rubber band; and I subscribed to Fitzgerald's notion of emotional bankruptcy, overlooking that he had decades and barrels of alcohol on me, because it was a relief to have some kind of theory. I'd read Raymond Chandler and I detect in my diary an imitation of certain passages from *The Long Goodbye*—the exchanges with the psychiatrist, the mythologizing of the doctor—which I used as a guide for life in a psychiatric hospital.

So the notion of being in a mental hospital was not entirely foreign. The boy had been hospitalized, as far as I knew, because he did things his parents didn't want him to do, like drinking alcohol or smoking pot. The girl was in her hospitals because she couldn't perform as a brilliant student anymore, because she couldn't stop crying, and cut her wrists and took massive doses of pills that were around the house because she was on a regime of drug therapy. Both ways of behaving sent you to a hospital.

I felt as though I had not earned being sent so suddenly and swiftly to the psychiatric ward of a hospital thirty blocks south of home. I had been suffering but the reason the adults wanted me there was because I had cut my finger. The suffering, which by that time had gained a momentum of its own, was a private mystery, one that I thought I would never solve. My father had no tolerance for my unhappiness. My stepmother didn't believe in looking back or in probing for secrets. She was pulling my father into their present and future. It must have been awful for her, eight months after their wedding, to find that the middle daughter of the trio she had no intention of mothering was causing more trouble than she or her new husband could handle.

It is the imprisonment and the terror and the betrayal I can't get over. I understand how much my father longed for and needed my silence, my acquiescence to his marriage, my exit from his new household, but letting me be hospitalized seems excessive. Up until the moment I was shown into my room, I expected that someone would intervene and stop my father from doing this to me. The only person who might have stopped him was my mother whose return I was still awaiting and I didn't mention her to a soul in that place, not even to myself, for fear that I would ruin everything.

❧

I was shown to a room with two beds in it and shocking-pink bedspreads covering the bed. Across the hall the beds were covered with turquoise spreads. The room was empty until my roommate was wheeled in on a gurney, limp from a shock treatment, and transferred to her bed by several nurses. She was from the Lower East Side, obese, Jewish, married, the mother of a boy, two, and a girl, nine. Her daughter had brought her comic books, her husband brought her *True Romance* magazines.

The woman who had been in my bed before me, Terésa, now had a single and sat during dinner swaying back and forth, saying, "Oh my dear God in Heaven, I don't know what to do."

The nurse said, "Finish your dinner, dear, then you can go to your room."

"I don't want to be alone."

I wrote in my diary, in red caps, *SILENCE.*

Later Terésa saw me reading *The Last Temptation of Christ* and took umbrage at the jacket copy: "He was terrified of death and lusted after women." She said that Gesthemene was bad but He was pure in thought, word, and deed.

Another patient's husband was spending $230 a week to keep her there, and he thought she wasn't trying hard enough.

I noted that I was the youngest person there.

One patient who became my friend outside of the hospital was in his thirties, an art dealer, a brilliant man who wore large eyeglasses. André had gone to college at age fourteen, he told me, and he was funny, wry, and kept rebounding to Tower Nine. He tried suicide. He drank too much. He couldn't function, a new word for me, a hospital word. I didn't wonder why he was there. I was just glad that he was.

When we both got out of the hospital, I visited him downtown in his apartment, which was filled with crisp art and sparsely but smartly furnished in a style I'd never seen before. I met him at his gallery in midtown and we went downtown in the subway together, then to the grocery store to buy ingredients for dinner. The cashier put the lettuce at the bottom of the paper bag and was about to put the meat on top when André began a tirade about what a stupid thing *that* was to do, and with *one* simple job to do why couldn't it be done right? I watched the tender greens being crushed, shocked at hearing his voice, suddenly the loudest in the noisy store.

At the hospital I was intrigued most of all by Vera who was wiry, dark, in her late twenties, her skin dull as if it covered an emptiness, a look I recognized from my friend who was beginning her career as a mental patient. She told me that her doctor said to her, *Cut the crap, Vera—don't hand me any of that shit.* She ordered a daiquiri one day when we were all led outside by an orderly for a field trip to a restaurant. She was actually served the drink and let me have some sips. Her act of defiance made me feel hard and sophisticated, but even I recognized that it was only more of Vera's crap, which might keep her in the hospital and guarantee her return. She had unsuitable affairs with married men, she told me, as if it were like smoking, a habit that led to trouble and that she would be hard pressed to relinquish.

I wrote about the other patients in my diary but I rarely recorded how I felt, and no wonder. I was too busy: smiling, making phone calls, writing letters, receiving visitors, waiting for letters and phone calls, wondering which boy I loved, being happy with the nightgown I wore, deciding to learn to weave in the art therapy room. I observed. I quipped in my diary. I tried to adjust, though I wondered what I was doing there with those people. I looked for a friend. Since I arrived there on a Friday, nothing was done except pills for sleeping until Monday, and the time dragged on. My stepsister brought me lilacs. I wrote, *First time I can look at them without being overwhelmed by Mommy dying. Oh stop it, stop it, stop it.*

The other patients frightened me those first days, both those who were obviously suffering and receiving treatment, and, far worse, those who seemed normal, like people on the outside, no bizarre behavior, no rocking back and forth, only a drugged look and an air of altered personality, of something gone wrong between the interior and exterior selves.

The second day I noted, *If there were only some kind of way out or in.* It was not only my growing habit as a writer that made me write down what the woman who had been swaying at dinner wore *(Friday Terésa wore navy blue, Saturday gray, today yellow)*, but that I had no capacity for understanding or articulating how I felt, only what I observed. I was fearful to be in the hospital, yet

I was aware that I needed to cooperate or I might be kept there a long time or sent somewhere worse. I never tried to escape, though it would have been easy when I walked my visitors to the elevator. The first days there I had no idea what to do or what would happen. Once the week began and the doctors returned I still had no idea of why I was there and what I was supposed to do now. I had, as in horrible math class, no way to solve the problem and no one to point out a solution so simple and clear that I would have to say—*Why didn't I think of that? Why didn't I know that all along?*

I grew more alienated from myself, for my feelings had landed me there, had they not? They were the mystery, they were the enemy. When they rose in the form of bad dreams and constant mumbling worry, what should I do but fear them, for look where they landed me, in a room with a slab of a woman who was having electric currents sent through her for some reason, with a woman who rocked back and forth for some reason and asked God for help and got none. Were they what I would become? Had they been me at one time?

I didn't consider my feelings, turn them over, shake them, hold them upside down, let them be, have their time and leave. I didn't understand them as a cycle that repeated, with or without external stimuli. I was a mystery to myself, a secret as if there had to be a secret, as if I had done something wrong to land in such a place because I had had some feelings. It took me years to figure out: It wasn't the feelings I was having that got me there, it was the actions I took. The world—father and stepmother, teachers, psychiatrists, school administrators—didn't care how I felt so long as I didn't act on my feelings. Once I did, my goose was cooked.

What were they all thinking of? When my sorrow went unnamed and unacknowledged as grief, it became habitual and took on a dimension and shape that was worse than mourning.

Doubleness became habitual: how I felt, what I wanted on one side; what I had to pretend to feel and want on the other.

Put on a happy face. Don't wear your heart on your sleeve. Don't ask your stepmother to be your mother, let her be herself and see if that self has something to teach you. Don't expect your father to do what he cannot do. Take care of yourself. No one else knows what you need but yourself. If you're tired, sleep. If you're hungry, eat. Get an education. Find some work to do in the world that interests you and provides a living. Love the worthy. Take a hint.

I knew no simple rules for getting along, and the adults I knew were of no help: my mother was dead, my father unavailable, and my stepmother was the last person I would have listened to even if she'd known what to say. Before my mother died, I'd liked my parents' friends, but now I rarely saw them and didn't think of turning to them for help. Without being told explicitly, I knew that my father would hate it if I spoke to any of them of my unhappiness.

In the hospital, I learned to distrust myself as if I were filled with demons that now and then put me at the mercy of adults. The hospitalization, logically, might have taught me to take care of myself, since no one else was about to do it. Instead, I became a stranger to my own best needs, and a guessing game ensued, as if I were the last to know my own feelings and desires. The shock of the sudden imprisonment prolonged my inability to do the simplest things: like myself, be loyal to myself, be kind. It is true for every adult that we must learn to be our own best parent. Long after I was finished with my stay at the hospital, I still waited for the adults around me—at home, in school, on the job—to be good parents at last. The waiting retarded my maturing and perpetuated the twilight of my childhood far too long.

On Monday there were blood tests and a physical exam, on

a regular hospital floor, which brought me back to my mother's illness. Now I was in the hospital gown. It was raining *Monday rain,* I wrote. Then I went back up to Tower Nine and started learning weaving. One visitor brought drawings, another, a bunch of books. Vera stumbled into the day room after two pills and she smoked and watched the news, utterly absorbed, which puzzled me. My doctor said that I would have more tests the next day, which I welcomed as distraction—*Anything.*

I was being given three doses daily of Thorazine, whose side effects were sleepiness, nausea, and a sensitivity to the sun. The pale spring sun of New York, which I was exposed to during brief periods on the roof or when we walked a few blocks to a neighborhood luncheonette for an official outing, did make my cheeks a little more flushed than usual. By the fourth day I noted that my headaches and feeling of nausea were gone, but the pills didn't seem to help my sadness and anxiety. It isn't any wonder that they didn't. It's testimony to my constitution or my unconsciousness that they didn't do more harm.

Thorazine is an anti-psychotic drug used on chronic schizophrenics. Neither my actions nor feelings were psychotic. I was, clearly, depressed, and Thorazine wasn't the drug for me. What I needed was therapy to help me through the years I still had at home and to understand my mother's death. My father, a mental health professional in a city full of psychiatrists and psychotherapists, found a bad doctor for me and then acquiesced to bad advice.

First day of May, rain. In my room a scent of flowers. In me three little pills. Didn't seem to help. The feeling of nausea is gone, headaches less frequent. Crying the next day, and *snotty to Daddy, uncooperative with Dr.*

I was allowed to go around the city starting on May 4, using the hospital as a base, freed as arbitrarily as I was first sent there. In the diary I talk about killing myself but then say I would never do it. The talk of suicide was a jab of energy or drama, a relief because I could understand that desire. I wrote that I would impose rules, that there had to be rules. I had lunch with friends from camp and became exhausted if I was out of the hospital too long, restless once I returned. The SATs loomed. On the doctor's advice I broke off my hospital friendship with Vera. On May 18, the doctor said I was fifty percent out of the woods, that I would feel up and down, that I should take care of myself. I stayed in the hospital for the weekend, taking the SATs and returning to the hospital, and then I was released. I didn't return to school right away but wandered around for a week or so. I lay on a hill in Riverside Park and read *The Magic Mountain*, my eyes scanning the lines so swiftly that I became breathless, holding the book before my face so that I needn't look around or feel a thing.

∽

When I left the hospital, I was on my own. I didn't realize that I had to take care of myself nor did I set myself to that task with insight and resolve. I only mean to say that I no longer trusted anyone. The lesson I learned was to lie and to obscure. I did it so well that after a while I had no idea what was bothering me.

I finished the school year, and I returned to camp that summer. I was a senior in high school and applied to colleges outside of New York which I had come to think was the source rather than the background to my trouble. In the decades to follow I was in and out of psychotherapy, some life-sustaining and some useless. I was never hospitalized again, but I fantasized about a refuge of a kind that the hospital wasn't.

No one—and I include myself—ever said: It is April 27 and in seventeen days it will be the third anniversary of your mother's death. No one noticed, no one anticipated, no one talked about what seems now like simple grief.

The house in New Jersey was lost to me forever when my father married Netty though he held onto the place for eight years, until 1969. That was a long time for a man who worried about money and was harassed by the surprises that a house produces in the form of disasters and maintenance. He didn't want me visiting it even when it was vacant, not that I suggested it often, for I was playing possum with my missing it. My favorite word for it became *irretrievable*. He was possessive of the house and prickly, burdened by it emotionally and financially. He evaded answering my questions about what the tenant was doing that was so terrible, what was the problem with the furnace, the roof, the paint job. When he said he was going to sell it, I begged him not to, saying that soon I would be grown up—five years at the most—and I would move to the house, live in it, and take care of it, if only he would keep it for me.

The closing date was supposed to be June 25, though negotiations dragged on until October. In an April note to my father the real-estate agent (a casual friend) wrote a p.s.: "You never did make that promised visit & now I guess you never will." This is one of two hints at what parting with the New Jersey property meant to my father. The other is in a letter, dated a few weeks later, from the same agent: "You spoke of an investment for your proceeds." He goes on to suggest "twenty to twenty-five acres of dry, level land, corner property in the Flockstown area with two streams that converge into one. It belongs to a farmer who has switched from milk cattle to beef cattle which require less pasturage. He has no longer any need for this field." The agent predicted great future potential for the land, "especially if divided," and he was right. Across from our house and the Downes's farm, the fields are full of houses.

In any case, there the paper trail of my father's possible investment ends.

By the time he sold the house in New Jersey, my stepmother had found and bought a house in the Berkshires. They had rented in the area for a few summers, and they had friends there. Tanglewood was nearby, Jacob's Pillow for dance, and Williamstown for theatre. They fixed up a studio for him and there, after retirement, he painted and worked on etchings. The Berkshires became an integral part of their life together, their place through the longer seasons that retirement permitted until his death. My stepmother then carried on with their routine, allowing few alterations in their pattern, making few allowances for her increasing age. The house in New Jersey was the past, his past without her and with my mother. My stepmother must have decided to stay well away from the matter of my father selling the New Jersey house. I recall no struggles of the type they had about other matters major and minor, with Netty urging my father to act, to do, and he deliberating, dragging his feet, stalling, and, as always, doing things on his own schedule. Perhaps she wisely resolved that he could spend his money and energy keeping the New Jersey place, but she was not participating. Off to Massachusetts.

The closest thing I have to a diary for this time are my father's figurings, the carbons of letters to lawyers and real estate agents, bankers and tenants, and the accounting when he sold the New Jersey house in 1969 of what he and my mother added to it from 1946 on. A bank appraisal described the outside of the house in 1961 as "sadly lacking in repairs and paint," though it notes a roof that appeared to be new. I can tell from the stapled-on addenda to the lease that my father had worried over every possibility of renting: if the tenant wanted the swimming pool to function, he had to fix it himself; the tenant could use the landlord's furniture; if the landlord wanted to

rent the schoolhouse, he would. There is much correspondence from the real estate (also my father's rental) agent who
had to chase the tenant up his private lane (our driveway) to get
the rent, current and arrears, and, at the end, a futile request
from my father for a missing gate-leg table that the tenants said
they'd never seen. I can imagine my father's sinking heart each
time fresh mail arrived from Long Valley and he had to attend
to insurance, repairs, maintenance, and taxes on a place that
had outlived itself.

It is my distinct memory that my mother's jars of jelly and
watermelon pickles were still on the shelves by the kitchen
door when I went to the house in Long Valley in 1969 to see if
there was anything I wanted. It was ten years after her death.
The place had been first unoccupied, then lived in by tenants,
so it seems unlikely that the jars of pickled watermelon rind
and grape jelly labeled in her round handwriting would still be
there, but I remember them, cobwebbed and grimy. I went out
to the house with my father's permission, though he acted as if
there were something there that I shouldn't see. I interpreted
this to mean that there was something I would harm in the
house. It might have been the opposite, and in his mistaken and
well-intentioned way my father still wanted to keep me from
mourning. Or, having decided to be rid of the house at last, he
felt that the decision was set for us all and regarded my wanting
to see it again as criticism.

I found the house easily, as if I'd been there only days before, but I was appalled by the signs both of disuse and another
family's occupancy. I scurried through the cold house as if I
had broken in. The house was a mess. It had changed without
me, and, no longer inhabited by us as we had been before my
mother's death, was no longer mine.

In the white-painted desk in my bedroom, I found the letters my mother had written me the last summer of her life,

when I was in Florida and off at camp. To my eternal regret I threw them away. It was an appalling thing to have done, but I recognize myself in the deed. Since her death, I had developed the capacity to sever connections with people and places. It was nothing to brag about or to be ashamed of; it was as involuntary as breathing and far less under control. I had no tolerance for the complexities of relationships with other people.

Why should I keep her letters, I wondered. Where would I keep them? I had no place for them, I insisted. I had no place for my feelings about missing my mother nor would I for years to come.

❧

I graduated from college in 1968, a year after my original class at Bennington, for I'd dropped out in the fall term of my sophomore year. I was then in love, I thought, with a boy who was himself a college drop-out living in New York, but I met another boy who went to a college nearby and I slept with him. With neither lover was sex the point. I felt some sensations and affection, I liked the feel of their bodies and their passion, but my real desire was to belong.

The first boy came up from the city for a visit, armed with the knowledge of my betrayal. He told me he never wanted to see me again and life became very simple in that moment. I walked away from him across the flat green lawn of the college, straight to my room where I swallowed all the aspirin I could find and cut my wrists, not horizontally but vertically, the way a friend said was really effective, the way you do it when you mean it.

I have wondered why I treated my life so cavalierly. I can't bring reason to bear on my action, only gratitude that I was inept and ended up, not dead or even injured but in the college infirmary.

I moved so automatically from being rejected by my boy-friend to being willing to die. I glided across the lawn, I wept in my room, I found my tools, I moved into the act, and why? I be-lieve that it was the triangulation that depleted me of hope, the particular problem of having two boyfriends, two attractions, and feeling pulled between them. For another girl, this might have been a moment to think out which boy she preferred and to make a choice. For me, it was a replication of the unbearable triangulations at home: I and my mother and my stepmother; I and my father and my stepmother.

When I was released from Roosevelt Hospital three years before, I left with no insight into myself, only a greater capacity to dissemble outwardly. My sadness seeded in the numbness I practiced and became morbid. The sadness ossified and took the place of understanding. My mother had died ages before, it seemed, and I couldn't understand why I would still feel sad about her. No one else mentioned her. I sought the reason for doubting any possibility of happiness, for feeling myself set apart from all my friends, only in the present and in myself as an individual. I had no family, I reasoned, so that could not be it. I was a mystery to myself and didn't know how to be in the world. At times I was furious, at times filled with burning hap-piness, and neither state could be traced to a source.

I took pride in not feeling physical pain or discomfort. Slowly but surely I desensitized my body and rid myself of the child who danced and skated. I was happiest with my body when it gave me no trouble, when I could pretend that it wasn't there.

Back in New York, I lived on the Lower East Side with the first boy, seeing a psychiatrist as a requirement of future re-admission to the college, and working at my first job in pub-lishing, learning a trade. This was a matter of luck.

The psychiatrist bored me and I believe that I bored him. I

worked at being opaque, inventing what to tell him in a session, and, as I rode the subway back downtown, I felt relieved if guilty for wasting my father's money once again. I fooled the doctor. I escaped with my secrets intact. If I knew little about myself, he knew even less, but I saw that he was in no position to hospitalize me. At the end of the winter, he gave me a clean bill of health and told me I could return to college in the fall.

∽

The summer I graduated, I found a job at a small publishing house that had its offices on University Place on the eastern edge of Greenwich Village. I found an apartment in walking distance of my job. A woman I worked with introduced me to an intern at Bellevue Hospital, and I liked him right away. He had grown up in Far Rockaway, had a brother who was also a doctor. Here was someone different from me, whose every move for the next few years was known and dictated.

I still have snapshots of us on our first weekend away at the beach where we stayed at a boarding house near Amagansett. I didn't understand how unusual it was for him to have a string of days off from the hospital or to be as relaxed as he was. He appeared whole to me, golden-skinned, handsome, happy-natured. "Will we be friends?" he'd asked after our first date. Of course. I believed that he was the man for me, and I wanted us to vault over the awkwardness of being new and to be settled and secure. I wanted him to change to suit my prejudices of the moment, so I persuaded him that psychiatry, for which I had no great respect, was more interesting than internal medicine, about which I knew nothing. I talked him into buying a Citroën instead of a car which he could get repaired. This much I did to him.

❧

My apartment wasn't bad and neither was the rent. The apartment's location at the crossroads of Greenwich Village on the corner of Bleecker and MacDougal didn't appear to be a liability until it was too late to get out. By day it had seemed to me to be part of the old Village—winding little streets and pretty buildings, Italians everywhere and the Blue Note up the street—but by night, weekdays and weekends alike, there was a carnival of noise and drunken tourists wandering the streets.

The building itself was old enough that the marble stairs, gray from a hundred years of dirt and washing with dirty water, were worn down at the center of each rise. My neighbors left their doors open to one another and as I climbed to my apartment I glimpsed their carved and brocaded furniture, some slipcovered in plastic; their mirrors veined in gold, hung on the bumpy plaster walls. The doors weren't open to me. I was a stranger, not Italian, not Catholic, but I wanted strangers. I had left the open skies of the Upper West Side to be different.

For a small apartment, there was lots of useless space. The first room was good for nothing but hanging my jacket on a hook and lining up a small collection of boots. The kitchen was a narrow afterthought and I slept in the next room—a passageway. In the living room I put two director's chairs and a marble topped bureau I'd found in Vermont. Next and last there was a closet that might have been a room. I imagined that I would put a desk in there and begin to write, but I was too restless and uncomfortable in the apartment, the building, the neighborhood, and my own skin to concentrate.

One evening I came home to find that a big rug was gone and all my jewelry, including the gold bracelet my mother had given me for graduating from elementary school. I still think of the bracelet sometimes at night, its flat links lying serenely in place. It didn't occur to me to move, though even after I had gates put up on the windows near the fire escape, I felt that anyone could get at me at anytime.

The intern should have passed from my life. The summer and the fall were full of promise but by winter we were tugging at one another. One cold night when he had said he wanted to be in his apartment by himself, I phoned him every half hour. That was as direct as we got in our quarrels—my clinging to the ringing phone, and his not answering it. By April, we agreed to stop seeing each other.

One night after work I developed a high fever that would not go away. I went uptown to the only doctor I knew, my mother's doctor, who sent me home to bed. The intern came back, and on the phone discussed with the doctor whether or not I had appendicitis. There was pain in my abdomen though not the rebound pain which occurs when pressure is applied, so my problem was not appendicitis. I grew more feverish, and I lost days in sickness and fever. The intern came by again. I talked on the phone to the doctor. The intern's face collapsed into an expression of worry, and I thought that he was afraid that I was trapping him with my sickness.

I went uptown in a cab to a gynecologist who diagnosed my problem as gonorrhea. I had pelvic inflammatory disease, he told me. An ovarian cyst had burst. My abdominal cavity was filled with infection. I had peritonitis. I was poisoned. Who, he asked, had I been fooling around with? No one but the intern. The gynecologist gave me an injection and slapped my naked buttock. He prescribed pills and told me that I would not feel well for days and that I wouldn't be able to work for another week. Come back, he told me, when you don't have a fever and we'll see what the infection's done to you.

～

As soon as the gynecologist said *ovarian*, all my powers of dis-association were called into action. I shut off and went back down into myself, allowing few words out, letting the sickness seal up my surface so that I might lie very quiet and still, so that I might die as I'd been waiting to since my mother had: *ovarian*. The infection had nothing to do with any possibility of cancer. The gynecologist might have explained that normal ovaries form cysts and that the cysts, if uninfected, go away of their own accord. If he did, I didn't hear. My ovaries were an explosion I'd been listening for, a rumble heard in the distance.

My fallopian tubes were put to the test when a radiologist sent liquid fire to them, pressure and fire, and the scar tissue held. I would continue to ovulate, I was told, continue to menstruate, but my tubes were thoroughly blocked. The eggs I would continue to produce could not be fertilized.

The intern explained that nights when he was at the hospital he'd been sleeping with another intern. Where? I asked. Not why, but where. She was the source of the gonorrhea.

Decades later, when I was closer to seeing what I'd lost through that infection, I passed the apartment building where he had his private psychiatric office on the ground floor. I wanted to toss Molotov cocktails through his windows. I wanted to burst into his office like water, like fire. I kept walking and envied him his wife, his possible children, his probable slobbering dog. I was a confirmed freak, shut out from his normality by my incapacity, by my damaged body, by my scars so deep inside that no one could see them.

～

Spring was when the bad things happened, my mother's death, my hospitalization, my infection. Now, my story was a turnabout of my mother's: her real disease and my non-disease; her real, surgical incision and my internal wound. My fate never to bear a child was linked with my separation from her. I never believed what the doctors said, that the scarring might be cut away, the tubes opened up.

One day when I was well again, I went uptown to visit my younger sister. I was thinking of moving uptown, back to the old neighborhood. We were walking on Broadway and Ninety-sixth Street, the crowded street on which I'd shuttled back and forth between my elementary school and home on Ninety-fifth Street. The light must have caught me in a funny way because Sarah stopped me and said, looking worried, "You're so thin. You're too thin." She was the only person who had noticed how altered I was by my illness. Here was recognition of what had taken place inside me, reassurance that I could be seen.

It took decades until I felt safe enough to cry. I wanted my mother so I could tell her that I couldn't have babies. She alone would have had the right tears to weep with me.

∾

The year after I graduated from college and worked for the publisher on University Place, I occasionally met my Aunt Molly for lunch. Sad for the loss of her sister, her only relative nearer than Georgia, and in the beginning of her own long decline, my aunt phoned at the office and invited me to lunch every month or so. My mother's sister was the only person I knew who talked about my mother, though Aunt Molly did not make the long journey from Yonkers to answer my questions or to tell me stories about my mother's life. It troubled Aunt Molly, and she could not stop it from troubling her, that she and my mother had quarreled about her child's not being invited to that birthday party in the year before my mother's death. I listened to her hopeless recital of the quarrel and the cause, and wished I never had to hear about it again.

For our lunches, I chose a corner restaurant, two blocks north of my office, a big Italian place, noisy with a high ceiling and tall windows. It had café tables on the street but we never cared to sit outside.

Invariably, I tried to tell Molly about my job. It was neutral ground and would divert her, I hoped. But she had her own subject, dear to her heart. Molly had decided that my father had killed my mother. Her death was his fault, and he had been the cause of the rift between the sisters.

For me, the guilty pleasure of hearing my mother's name was reason enough to meet my aunt for lunch. I would ask her about my mother in childhood, in adolescence, before she left Atlanta. Molly would tell me of my father's reluctance to allow my mother to see her own sister. My stepmother too was implicated in my mother's death. Time was pooling for Molly as it had for me.

The restaurant we always went to was not a fancy place, but I worried that it was too expensive since Molly always insisted on paying for lunch. That was my sanest thought. Neither of us sitting beneath the garlands of empty Chianti bottles and plastic grapevines was quite in her right mind.

Occasionally, I ventured uptown to the old neighborhood to have dinner with Daddy and Netty. I arrived by six for a drink before dinner, and talked to Daddy and Netty about my job. They were delighted that I was working in publishing, and they were quick to advise me on work problems, and to listen to office gossip and jokes that didn't travel well. At the end of one dinner, Daddy walked me to the subway, and I told him that I'd seen Molly. I told him what she'd said about Mommy's death, to warn him as if her thoughts might bring him harm. He said that Molly had troubles of her own and that she had always adored her sister.

I told my younger sister also. She was in music school by this time, with an apartment of her own in the neighborhood. She looked at me sideways, as if I had invented the idea, and asked why Molly thought Daddy had killed Mommy. When I couldn't answer coherently, we talked about something else.

I came to dread my aunt's phone calls to make a date for lunch. I always promised her at the end of our lunches that I would call to make the next date, but I never did.

In my old dream about my mother, I am walking up Ninety-fifth Street toward her. She is standing with her shopping cart, and catches sight of me. She sees me before I see her. She watches me approach.

At the end of the lunches with Molly I turned away and kept walking until I was sure she had begun her own progress. Then, I stopped, turned, and watched her limp down the block toward the subway, plagued by her bad back, which made her old before her time. I wanted to run after her, make her turn to me so that I could say words I didn't have to heal her wounds.

∽

I grew sick of New York after a few years of changing jobs and apartments. I wanted to be in the country to write, to concentrate, to drink good water, to breathe pure air. I was tired of feeling crowded and threatened. I had stopped going to museums and concerts and movies, so why stay in the city? I had my reasons for leaving, and so did a lot of other people at the time. The country was full of people like me, fleeing from the city and their families, but they lived in groups or couples and I was on my own.

I lived for a while in a farmhouse a friend owned in upstate New York, on the top of a hill with a view to the farms and hills below. In a landscape of fields, farms, and patches of woods, groups of Holsteins moved across the meadows and hills. It was dairy country, like the Schooley's Mountain of my childhood. I felt at home and claimed the area emotionally as mine, the place I would stay forever, and I decided I needed a place of my own. I had reasons: for the rent I paid, I could own a house. Why be obliged to a friend when I could be independent? I looked at an eighteenth-century house in a nearby village and decided against it, then a neighbor told me that a place down the hill was for sale, down the hill and around the bend, a place I'd passed a thousand times as I drove to Battenville to see my painter friends or to Salem to the pottery commune.

The house was at the end of an unpaved lane, past the asphalt-shingled house visible from the road. It was on a hill above Fly Summit, a settlement of a trailer and a few very small houses, near County Road 74 or Railroad Bed. At one time a trolley ran along the road, taking passengers from outlying farms to the nearby town of Greenwich, and one of the stops was Fly Summit. I had glimpsed the little white house and its barn, and assumed that both were part of the first house. Mostly as I drove past I looked out the other way across the fields and above Railroad Bed to the farms of Easton.

My neighbor drove me down the hill. Between the house and a little barn or garage was mud, and in it a few pick-ups were parked. The owner showed us the house. He was around my age, trying to be a rock musician. Until he and his wife bought it, the place had been in one family, so far as he knew, and the house, he thought, dated from the 1860s. The property was triangle-shaped and consisted of about nine acres: a pointed, sloping field (wet year round from underground springs); an old apple orchard; and one big field of almost five acres hayed by neighbors who lived in the house by the road. He and his wife were getting a divorce. The place was a dream gone by, he said, pointing in the melting snow and mud to the place where the summer before they'd planted their vegetable garden.

The siding was clapboard, white until you looked closely. There was not a curve or fret or extra piece of material made into ornament anywhere in the house, inside or out, with the exception of three lightning rods spaced across the peak of the roof, made of twisted iron and lavender glass globes. The garage was utilitarian, dirt-floored, with a work bench and just enough room for one car. The barn was big and built into the hill, with several stalls down below the hay loft which had a valley view over the five-acre field.

Inside, the rooms were small and the ceilings not especially high. The plain-papered plaster walls were broken where doorknobs had hit and in some other places where someone might have struck deliberately. In the front room, there was a poster of Jimi Hendrix crisscrossed with motorcycle chains, and a bamboo couch with no cushions; a chainsaw sat on the floor. The wooden floors were rough and uncarpeted, layers of paint and shellac outlining where over the years there had been rugs. The floors could be sanded, I calculated, and the walls painted white. Remembering my parents splatter-painting their way out of the house in New Jersey, I wasn't dismayed at the work ahead.

As we were leaving, the owner gave us the name of his real estate agent in town, and mentioned that a couple from Troy were interested in it for their son. They were thinking of offering twenty-nine thousand. I said, joking, that I'd give him thirty. I had no idea how to buy a house.

Alone that evening in my friend's farmhouse, I thought about the house down the hill. It struck me as significant that the whole triangular property had been there all along and I had never known it, yet it appeared when I needed it. I felt comfortable in the house and outside, walking to the barn, standing and looking at the place where the garden had been.

By the middle of the night I saw that I was risking the equilibrium of the present. I might not be happy exactly, but I was working. I had finished one novel. It was with an agent in New York, and I had started another book. I had a reasonable way to make a living and could live where I wanted. Every day was mine to write, though that time felt often like a vast empty space that I must crawl through to reach the night. I wanted the complications of what I saw as a real and complete life, as my other country friends had theirs: gardens and houses and cars that broke down. Still, I was risking my ease of motion. I would be tied down to the house, responsible for it and the work it needed.

In the days that followed, I looked at houses that were prettier, had more land, needed less work, but none of them would do. The little house felt like the place where I should be—not too far away from where I was already used to living, not on a strange road.

Then the figurings began, rows of numbers on pieces of paper: how to get a down payment, how to pay the mortgage, how to pay for the repairs that a closer look told me would be necessary before I could live there. Years later, when I looked through my father's files on buying the house on Schooley's Mountain, I recognized myself in his many pages of nervous calculations.

Knowing nothing about debt, I borrowed enough to buy the house and spent five years making it livable. It needed so much and I had only enough to make an initial run at the first-floor repairs.

The closing was in May, and the first summer I slept on the porch, listening to the amazing cacophony you didn't hear from inside: frogs, birds, owls, and cows, and every so often the desperate cries of the neighbor's peacocks. A friend worked all summer to preserve the plaster downstairs. Sheetrock is modern and geometric, while even the studs in the walls were irregular and organic, hand sawed, so that he had almost to sculpt the two materials together. He spent days nose to nose with the wall, sanding patiently and with such skill that it was impossible to tell where the Sheetrock ended and the plaster began.

I decided to move the kitchen to the walk-through room and consolidate the house in the old portion heated by the oil furnace. I found three windows at a junkyard, and a carpenter arranged them with the arched one in the center, giving the view a vaguely religious frame and the room much more light. Once the sink, counters, and open shelves were installed, I could see out while I washed dishes. I took the doors between the front room and the new kitchen to a stripper in Vermont and when they were bare wood, I waxed them. I bought a big freezer from Sears and practically fell into it, each time I reached for some frozen berries.

I wrote fiction in the mornings, working on an editing job for a foundation in Texas in the afternoons, a job that lasted for my first few years in the country. When my back hurt from hours of sitting at my work table, I went upstairs and hung by my hands from the bare rafters, hoping to straighten my cramped muscles. If I was restless, I might go outside and split wood or cross-country ski in the winter, trying to get warm and tired enough to write again.

On occasion, I had to travel back to New York City for research or to Houston for meetings, but it became increasingly difficult for me to leave my house. There was nothing human keeping me there, nothing alive but the three cats my neighbors fed while I was gone. There were sheep in the meadow—my neighbor's teenage son's—but I had no duty to them. Yet every time I left—for the airport or to go to town ten miles away—I had to turn back to be sure the place was all right without me. I prepared excitedly for the shortest trip to town on the dimmest of errands, rushed through the door, stood for a moment between house and truck, and wanted nothing more than to be back home, for the time to have passed and to be again safe at home. It wasn't only my safety that worried me, it was the safety of the house and what might happen without my vigilant presence. It had stood for a hundred years without me, but now, I felt, might fail in my absence. Perhaps the fire in the wood stove would escape or I'd left something cooking on the electrical stove. Perhaps any unforeseen thing might happen through my forgetfulness. I was anxious when away from the house on a local errand, and the anxiety bloomed when I was away from the area altogether. The feeling of being wrong and in the wrong place spread like spilled wine when I could not obey it and return to the house. My anticipation of being inside the house on the correct side of my door, had the pull of desire.

Evenings in the winter, I turned on the radio and listened to the news from the public radio station in Albany. I drank a glass of wine while I cooked and prepared more food than I needed, cooking each night as if I had a family to please. I set a place at the table and read as I ate, always eating too quickly so that the meal was over too soon and I had the night before me. Once it was completely dark, I could settle down, but there was a moment each night just before dark when I considered leaving, driving to town, anything to keep the day in motion.

I read a good deal, of course. I felt impatient for each new day and burdened by it. I was terrified that I would waste my time, and also felt that my time was useless for I was alone and it mattered so little to anyone else what I did. I took trips into New York to check footnotes on the book I was copy-editing, and the trips scared me, as if I wouldn't be allowed to return to my house, yet when I did return, the moment I was inside I realized that I'd rushed back to an empty house.

When visitors came for the weekend, I spent days getting ready for them, cleaning the house and driving all over the countryside to gather meat from the butcher on Railroad Bed, Jersey milk from Mr. Calhoun in Hoosick, and sometimes as far as Bennington for wine. Fridays felt like the day when we would go to Gladstone to pick up my father, the discomfort of change and the excitement of it too. When my visitors left on Sunday afternoon, I was left lonely and cranky, thinking I had been too eager for a visit. Now I was alone again and mostly glad for it.

It is hard, years later and many miles away, not to condescend to myself as I was then, not to forget the rush of love and promise I felt when I lived in my house. Freud said that melancholia seeks mania, and I had found a resting place for both emotions. I had found a way to save myself, I felt, for that was the urgency with which I undertook to buy my house and to live in it.

I was twenty-seven. I seemed finally to be in motion, frantic motion, to get the money to buy the house, to fix it up enough to live in it the first winter, to continue my improvements, to write my books and stories there. I seemed by will alone to be propelling myself into an unknown future. I wanted to be a writer and to have my work published. I wanted to be in love and to be loved; this much I could say aloud. I couldn't say that I wanted a child or that I wanted to have my mother with me again; that I wanted more than anything through my determined forward motion to go back and be once more with my mother in the country.

I didn't understand why I wasn't happier. I lived in a place whose beauty matched my idea of the beautiful. It was a landscape of natural grace tempered by human beings at their best in the old wooden buildings, simple and well-sited, and in the farms. Yet the beautiful sights left me feeling out of place, as if I should stay quiet so that my unnecessary and alien presence wouldn't be noticed. If it was a very good day, I felt at one with the farmers and their unceasing activity, but my conceit never lasted long.

After I had been in my house two winters, I began to sell stories about country life, and each story sold meant more work to the house. I wrote one story while the carpenter built counters and shelves in the kitchen ten feet away. In time the house had new wiring, Sheetrock, and paint. The big back room was Sheetrocked and heated by a Norwegian stove, with back-up for only mildly cool spring days from an electric heater I hardly used because I feared the electric bill. I bought cords of wood and split it for the stove, feeling inauthentic because I wasn't gathering wood myself from my own woodlot.

At moments—gardening, cooking, splitting wood, writing—I felt free of myself, as if I were possessed or someone else. This freedom I called being myself, finding myself, doing what I was meant for, my true nature, in my true place, country life at last. It was an imitation, so deeply felt that I didn't know what I was doing, of my mother and her happiness at being my mother, working on her old house, up on the ladder painting the trim.

When I'd applied to the local bank for a mortgage, I'd been asked to write a letter explaining why a young woman would want to bury herself in the country. I'd answered that I needed quiet to write, that I'd gone to college nearby and had friends in the area. I wrote what I needed to convince them that burying myself was not my goal, but of course it was. I wanted to be there, faithful to the house, faithful to the place, rejecting all other places and lives. I began to see a future for myself, to see myself as someone who in her youth took on a large and unlikely project and who would stay loyal to it, doing what she could each day, sticking it out, waiting it out—but what it was I waited for I kept a secret from myself.

From the beginning, I hoped that if I stuck it out, then one day my life would be changed utterly and remain the same. The house on its triangle of land would be polished, landscaped, a masterpiece, but it would be the same place I'd found. I was not waiting for a man to marry or to rescue me, although I was lonely. What I wanted was to reverse the bad luck which had brought my mother's death and would, most likely, kill me in turn. Triumph over that fate would come in the form of the happiness of work and home. Often when I walked up the slope past the end of the road and onto the muddy track that was my own land, into the barn to look out over the five-acre meadow to the road and the sweep of farms beyond, I imagined being buried there after a life of steadiness and fidelity. My feeling of expectancy as I walked to the barn, as if I might find the changed life there or emerge from the barn to see the change waiting for me, is one I can recall viscerally to this day. The fantastic hope came back no matter how many times I took that walk.

One winter day after I was thirty, when nothing had changed though the house looked a lot better and I was a published writer, it occurred to me that I would have a different life, that I'd feel less useless and alone, with a child. I wondered if I wanted the child so that I would have someone to inherit the house, someone to bury me in the field. I remember where I was when I thought of her—on the couch in the living room. I had my thought and examined it, so unlike my usual round of thoughts about money and time to write. I almost saw her before me, and I was almost able to feel my connection to her. I told no one about it. It was not an idea about having a child from my body but about being a mother, about the child at the center of my life. The physical child was small and dark. She wore overalls and stood looking at me. It was afternoon. I never told another soul, and I didn't analyze what having such a fantasy might so obviously mean—that I wanted a child of my own.

I lived in my house for six years altogether, and then I left that life.

For all that I had done there, my house was a parallel house, never itself alone, and my life there was parallel to the time when my parents were happy in New Jersey. In the end, I left because the beauty of the countryside could not touch my melancholy. It became part of my melancholy, a reproach to my restlessness. When the sun came through the front window I saw the view up the hill and I saw the simple room, the beauty of the bubbly old glass, and there was serenity in that moment. In the next moment I waited for something else to happen, and the particular interruption I sought never came.

I didn't say this as I prepared to leave. I said that I would be back the next summer, that I was taking an editorial job in Texas for the money to support the house. The strain of money was interfering with my work, I said. No sooner did I begin a story than I began to worry if it would sell, and this was fatal for writing, I said, feeling melodramatic. I was as scared as I had ever been. In leaving Fly Summit, leaving the East altogether, I was making a change so fundamental that it felt as if a part of my body were being ripped away. In October 1978, I made the drive to Texas, my Pinto wagon filled with clothing, books, rugs, and a blanket chest that was made from six pieces of pine from an old forest.

∽

In Texas, summer lasts until the first norther at Halloween, and during the hot Sundays of the fall of 1992, I put my son in his stroller and walked to the elementary school playground close to our house. We lived in a quiet town that grew even more silent after church when everyone, it seemed, Protestant and Catholic alike, was at home, eating their Sunday meal.

Solomon would soon be three and he was giving up taking naps. Some Sundays I'd put him in his car seat and we'd drive out into the country, watching for favorite oil pumps or fields, the pink farmhouse and the peach orchard near the river. Sometimes we would stroll toward the square to look at the Victorian courthouse that resembled a big Polish church and visit the fire engines which Solomon climbed on and pretended he was driving, from the biggest, newest one to the 1911 antique that he called the baby because it was so much smaller than the others. Most often we went to the playground.

When I was a child, I looked at my mother and Faith Morgenstern, at other mothers of my friends, women who were in their thirties and forties, and thought how beautiful they looked and how complete their lives seemed. I always wondered how to get from here to there, from childhood to that middle age of motherhood and marriage. Now I was in the middle of my forties, with a child and a husband and a house in this small Texas town thirty miles south of Austin.

I met my husband soon after I moved to Houston. I was a senior editor at a city magazine, and he was starting out as a journalist. I'd decided the summer before I met Joel that I had no talent for love and would never again look for a lover. Not looking, not seeking, I found him. Slowly I began to trust him and to see that he had no intention of bringing our relationship to a quick end. We formed an intimate companionship, and our possible future didn't take over from our actual present. Often I felt retarded in the first few years I knew him, like a wild child who had developed in isolation from other human beings.

We married in 1981 and after living in Houston, Dallas, Galveston, and Austin, settled in Lockhart in 1984. We wanted a five-bedroom house since we were both freelance writers then and needed offices at home, although, as soon as we bought the house, he got a job working for the State of Texas and I got a teaching job at the University of Texas at Austin.

Our house in the town of Lockhart had been the victim of a family fight. Built for a doctor at the turn of the century, it had at first been one story with a generous attic, then upstairs rooms were added in the 1940s with their own voluminous attic. The ceilings were high, the floors downstairs a special hardwood, but the place had been neglected for years. We were told that the woman who had last lived there, the stepmother of the family, hadn't wanted to repair the house which would go, at her death, to her stepchildren, and they hadn't cared to put money into the house where she lived. The roof had failed and hadn't been replaced. The wallpaper had peeled from the walls and the house smelled of mold.

My own family had always seemed to me like a letter puzzle, plastic squares locked in a form, slick on the bottom so you can move them around. You get three rows right but the fourth is wrong no matter what you do. The house we bought was a material demonstration of such family trouble.

We had found the house one day when we were living in Austin and went to Lockhart for its famous barbecue. Driving around, we noticed the house for sale, though the sign was nearly hidden by the overgrown lawn. We had the foundation repaired, the plumbing and electricity replaced, the walls Sheetrocked over the ruined wallpaper. We painted inside and out, then hand-waxed the floors downstairs and painted the upstairs floors barn red. Seven years later the downstairs was reconfigured to make the big kitchen more functional and to add a new bathroom and a closet in our bedroom.

For the seven years we lived in Lockhart, up until we adopted our son, it often seemed that we were perching there.

We didn't go to church and didn't have a child to send to the local schools. We hadn't grown up there and didn't work in the town. Most of my days, though, were spent there, in my house and our garden in the back yard, jogging around the high-school track, and it afforded me much of the same quiet, distant life I had in Fly Summit. I had already written a novel set in Houston and had immersed myself in its atmosphere and people. In Lockhart I came to know an old man who lived on his farm some miles out of town. He taught me about wildflowers, and through him I met other people living in the area. I learned about rural Texas through them. The east was the past, I thought, and Texas was the present. If it was Manhattan, May 1959 in my dreams, in my waking hours I knew where I was.

We'd married knowing I couldn't bear a child, but that became far less important than the fact that we wanted to be parents. I had long since accepted that I would never be a mother, so deeply accepted the idea that it seemed that my deprivation came not because of the infection that had closed my fallopian tubes but because I was meant never to have a child, had never been capable of having a child, not by nature or body, as if I had never been another way before the infection, or as if the ovarian cancer that overtook my mother had also taken away my body. Now, it seemed, none of that mattered. The point was the child and the family we might become, and we were very lucky. Our son was placed with us at the end of October, and we brought him home to Lockhart on November 8, 1989, when he was twenty-three days old. He changed everything in our lives.

I became a person whose eyes were open for the first time. I had the companions of my heart. I had a new ability to speak to strangers, to see the world rosily. Daddy and Netty soon visited and my father called Solomon a "merry old soul." Netty counseled me to take care of myself, to keep time for myself. Our life in the town changed. People who hadn't seemed to see me before, spoke to me, charmed by the sudden baby. In the grocery store, the cashiers asked how that baby was if he wasn't with me and greeted him if he was. I made more sense to them. Things in the world that I had thought were sentimental or lies, now gained meaning. For the first time since 1959, Mother's Day came without anger.

Without words, without anything but his own intelligence, beauty, and openness to the world, my fearless baby changed every day. He needed me in a direct, unmediated, and passionate way. What he needed I could give him and I did, and so I changed too, into a grown person in the world who had responsibilities and carried them out, who made decisions for her child and saw them through, who could care for someone else completely.

During the infant nights of frequent feedings or pacing with the baby to get him back to sleep, days when I walked him around the little town, I began to recall my mother as a living mother of young children, both as my mother when I was a young child and as I must have observed her with Sarah. She had once been a living woman who had her own way of doing the same things I was doing now, and she became part of my daily exterior life as she had been in the interior. I began to see what it must have meant for her to be so ill that she couldn't care for us any longer, and to know that no matter what she did she would have to leave us. She was not Aida Major after all and had not chosen to leave. A black wave had overtaken her and pulled me under also.

Daddy and Netty, too, were changed for me. They came more often to visit us in Lockhart to see the baby. We met them in Washington, D.C., when I read there, and they came for

Solomon's first birthday and witnessed him eating his first bite of chocolate. We visited them in the Berkshires in the summer.

When Solomon was two, my parents came on a visit, and my father looked pale, uncomfortable, slow, and very tired. He was in his late seventies, and traveled with a pharmacopoeia of ointments for his sensitive skin, allergy pills, antacids, sleeping potions. An inhaler was as much part of his luggage as his electric shaver. I'd come to interpret his health complaints as a defense against the world that troubled him and also against serious disease.

In the following spring, he had an operation for stomach ulcers that were not ulcers but stomach cancer, and he was given a year and a half at the most to live. I wanted to be in New York, to do whatever I could for him, but I learned another lesson: my family in Lockhart came first; Joel and Solomon, and the present had to be chosen over the past. I went as often as I could and came to appreciate that my father had been in my life as long as I had memory. He had watched me when I was my son's age, and he was the last witness. I realized that though I had brought him pain, he had always loved me and that I had also brought him pleasure. When I visited I tried to thank him for being my father and for always doing everything he could for me. He told me there would be more.

My father's illness laid bare my stepmother's devotion to him, and her strength and determination to do what she considered right. Twice in his life my father had found women who loved and cared for him. I had seen his second marriage before objectively, that is, for what it was in their lives, nothing to do with me, a happy marriage, but this was the first time I saw it without pain and with gratitude.

During one of my visits to New York, we were alone in the apartment while Netty ran some errands. We went into the kitchen and sat at the old Formica table where Anna Mae had sat leafing through the *Daily News.* My father told me that the sixtieth reunion of his class at Columbia was taking place in a few days. I asked him if he wished to go, thinking this was something I might help him do, but he asked, "Who would I know there?" It was true that his favorite classmates were his lifelong friends, and he knew where they were, one way or another. Then he said, "After a while it's all memory," and he quoted somebody (he didn't remember who'd said it) to the effect that after a while you prepare yourself for death through memory. I had been waiting through his illness for him to say the word *cancer,* to acknowledge death. Now he was surprising me.

"Is that how you feel now?" I asked.

He looked at me as if he were astonished that he'd raised such a stupid child. "You'll notice that I've curtailed my normal round of activities," he said.

Later, we were in the living room, reading the Sunday *Times,* and he fell asleep on the couch that had been in Brooklyn Heights, the one where I'd hidden, waiting to hear his footsteps coming up the stairs. It was covered by the slipcover my mother had made for it. When he woke, he smiled and said he was glad I was there. "You're good for me, like a racehorse who has a pet to help him relax."

When I said goodbye to my father on my last trip, three weeks before his death, I told him I wished I could stay a few days longer. At the moment of departure, I would have given a lot for another five minutes. My father said he wished that I could stay forever.

ॐ

My sisters and I had taken a great deal of trouble to come together on an October weekend in 1992, in the apartment on West End Avenue, in the room that was Sarah's childhood room and my father's in his old age. Valerie had come from Europe where she'd been living for many years, and I from Texas. Sarah still lived in New York. Netty had been in the Berkshires since a few weeks after his death, and was preparing to return to the city, probably the next day. He had died in that room, on June 9, the fifty-second anniversary of his marriage to our mother, and the room had to be cleared—the clothes packed up to be taken away, the papers bundled and destroyed, and the painting studio he had built into a corner of the room disassembled. Netty wanted to make it into a guest room. It would have been painful for Netty to pass by and see his bedside table, for example, piled as it was still with his alarm clock, his watch, the pills and the Kleenex, a flashlight, his small radio, his hearing aid, and, on the shelf beneath, his books and magazines.

The table was an old TV stand, metal tubing whose gilt had worn off in most places, with a top my father had jerrybuilt from a piece of pressboard. I had seen it for years and never realized how tippy and annoying it was. It made me want to go home and throw away anything in my house that half-worked, any chairs too frail to be sat upon, anything that I felt reluctant to spend money to replace, anything that would do in a pinch.

My father's desk—the one he had from the first apartment on Ninety-fifth Street on—was a work of art, his least self-conscious and most personal creation. Once he died, his formal art came alive; that is, his presence in his drawings and paintings was more evident than before, at least to me, but the desk had always been intensely himself. He made the desk, elementary carpentry, and in time rigged a drawing board on top, tilted permanently, held open by the top drawer, and layered it with piles of current and past bills and letters, newspaper clippings, drawings, a little chest of drawers for pencils, pencil knife, erasers, charcoal sticks, until the whole surface was covered and covered again. The right-hand drawer was open permanently, and often stacks of papers, manila file folders, or pads of lined paper were set on top of it so that to sit at Daddy's desk was to be enclosed by his papers. The desk drawers were so crowded that you had to shove in your hand to retrieve a file folder. No one else but Daddy could find anything on the desk. That was the point.

In many years, my sisters and I had been together only once, a few months before to celebrate our father's eightieth birthday. Now we had this one day together, just the three of us. We made a place for ourselves in the center of the room, with the bags for Goodwill containing his clothing all around us, piles of books that we wanted in the corners. Our mother's wooden jewelry box was in the center of our circle, and we opened it and divided everything in it.

We who agreed about very little had no quarrels about the division. I took a canoeing medal from Camp Iroquois 1921, and one from New Utrecht High School 1927, third place in the 220 yard dash. My great prize, which neither sister wanted, was a medal given in 1929 by the Pittsburgh Post-Gazette to Minnie Airov, Cambria District, Champion, Sixth National Oratorical Contest. I kept also a covered wagon charm that I recognized from my days as a cowgirl in New Jersey when I twirled my six-shooter in back of the house. I found and took home with me a yellow felt bookmark on which I'd used sequins and glue to spell out MOMMY. A few pieces of costume jewelry and an old-fashioned watch went to Valerie. Sarah got our mother's silver brooch, and we gave her the wooden jewelry box and the china that we'd always used for Seder.

In the middle of our sorting and dividing, we heard the front door of the apartment open and Netty's familiar, "Woo-hoo."

In the years since my father's death, I developed a fantasy

that if only Netty had not chosen to come home early from the country, we might have gone on to recapture a unity as sisters we'd never really enjoyed. We completed our division of the sacred objects hurriedly, and cleared up the room. That little scene of us on the floor of our dead father's bedroom—so primitive, so basic—seems to me the end of us as a family.

I carried as much as I could on the plane home, and shipped the rest. When my boxes arrived in Texas ten days later, one plate was broken from the set that my parents had ordered from the old man by the side of the road in the Pisgah Forest in 1941, on their way to Georgia to see her family. The dishes were glazed white on the inside, deep green on the outside, and each on the bottom was stamped with his insignia and the words "Pisgah Forest," and the year. The old potter had mailed the dishes to them—he'd not had a whole dinner set commissioned before—and they'd arrived safely in New York, then had survived the moves from Brooklyn to Ninety-fifth Street, two apartments there and then West End Avenue. By 1992, there were just enough dishes for each of us to have a cup, saucer, bowl and plate. I'd packed mine carelessly, hurriedly, like a thief.

∾

The spring before my father died, I had a laporoscopy to inspect an ovarian cyst that turned out to be normal, and my doctor had videotaped the procedure. There, he showed me a few days later at his office, circling with his ball-point pen on the little monitor—there were my fallopian tubes, covered with scar tissue, like little fists, just as he'd described them. My ovaries were tiny. He pointed out the present cyst and showed me old scarring on the ovarian surface. Then the angle of the camera changed and there on the screen was my liver, dark brown and shiny, just like a calf's liver, reassuringly healthy. I stayed and watched the tape again by myself. My inside that I had feared for so long would kill me, my dark and mysterious inside, was there before me, visible, measurable, not the stuff of dreams but living tissue. I felt whole, not the person, the writer, the mother and wife, friend, sister, daughter, trapped in this separate body, but a whole creature, one body, soul, and spirit.

◈

Before Solomon could walk or crawl, we drove into Austin to swim at Deep Eddy, a large pool filled with cold spring water mixed with city water. It lay along the Colorado River, shaded by enormous sycamore trees. The children's area descended from three inches to three feet five inches, and Solomon loved the water. I swam there alone also, when I could.

Immediately after my father's death, I felt completely relaxed only when I was underwater at Deep Eddy. I wanted to think, I wanted to remember, and it was very important for me to be sure of how I felt. Outside of the water there was, of course, always interference to my meditation, for Joel, Solomon, and I made a little puzzle of our own, moving around time, needs, and duties.

My most unexpected feeling was one of relief. My father's suffering had ended. There would be no more news now, no more announcements that the cancer had reached this far, that far, causing new havoc. All threats were past.

My father had always been there and now he was not. Cool, empty air accompanied me instead of a father. I thought often of his unoccupied body as I had seen it the day of his death. He would not haunt me. He was gone. Perhaps, as my younger sister believed, he was on his way to another life that had nothing to do with us.

The strain I'd felt for decades was also relieved. I had done my best to play my part as daughter in the family charade but now that was over. I didn't feel guilty for feeling relieved, though I told no one the word.

I also caught an inkling of something I hadn't seen before: a lifetime had gone by. My father's marriage to Netty had lasted thirty-one years.

❧

There were periods of present noise when I couldn't hear the sadness of the past and didn't think of times so irrevocably gone, and there were periods of intense quiet when Joel and Solomon receded, when all I could do was to give myself over to thinking hard about the past.

I found an article in a magazine about two women who painted semi-junky furniture white, all shades of white. I studied their method as though I were about to wet down a wooden lamp, let it go damp, apply acrylic paint, rub it off, wax it. I stared at the pictures of white furniture in a yellow room as if there were a secret message I had to decode.

One morning before dawn, Solomon woke up crying from a dream and when I went to him, he wanted me to stay. As I waited for him to go back to sleep, I thought of my mother and father going to the big country auction every Saturday, the crowded smoky auction where I feared being lost among the big-bellied, big-booted grown-ups. They must have worked hard to entertain us while paying attention to the goods for sale. My parents bought furniture there and painted it white, though they didn't wet it first and wax it after. For the room with the ballerina wallpaper, my mother had painted the desk with the fold-down top white enamel inside and out. Mirror frames and side tables were painted white, and the piano bench and child's coat rack now in my younger sister's apartment, painted white still. I had a double memory of me painting furniture in Fly Summit and Lockhart. Now there's my mother out on the flagstone patio, newspaper beneath the furniture, or out on the driveway, newspapers sticking to the newly painted furniture when the wind blows by.

I had questions for my mother about how to raise Solomon and I could never ask them. I'd worked hard to gain domestic knowledge without her. I wished for my mother to see Solomon, to delight as I did in him. I also began to understand how much time had passed since her death. By now she would have been eighty, and she might have died a natural death. Missing my father was not so consuming as missing her, nor as frustrating since I had a fund of memories and I'd had the chance to change my mind about him over and over again. My love for my mother remained that of a child for her mother. I missed her as Solomon said he missed me when he fell asleep at nap time.

Walking with Solomon to the fire station or to the playground, I passed bungalows like the one in Atlanta where my mother had lived, and I heard many of the sounds she might have—the crunch of pecans underfoot in fall, the winding chorus of cicadas in summer. I was approaching my forty-seventh birthday. She never saw hers.

Solomon asked me about time and death as we walked to the playground. *Why was Grandpa dead? Didn't he take his medicine? Was I sad? Was I going to die too?*

I sat by the flagpole, watching him play. I intended to play with him but I always ended up at the flagpole, his energy outlasting mine. I did nothing in particular, but I must have looked a certain, growingly familiar way, because Solomon came up to me and asked, "Are you sad? Do you miss your daddy?" I was asking my own questions. What would become of Solomon if I died? Joel had chosen me, but who might come next? I had almost fourteen years of knowing that I was completely loved by my mother, and that knowledge was my fundamental security.

How many years would my son have to understand that I'd loved him? My awareness of death was familiar but I feared what my dying might be for him. I had everything to live for. Now I needed to find a way to do it.

∾

Over the years, I'd talked to my gynecologist about prophylactic surgery. He'd done an exploratory laporoscopy when I was in my early forties to see what the chances were of opening my tubes, and we'd decided against taking the slim chance of opening the tubes and being able to carry a baby to term. He'd had another few looks for one reason or another. As far as he could tell, I was healthy, but I couldn't shake the idea that ovarian cancer was coming. He couldn't reassure me that it wasn't.

We were doing everything that could be done at the annual exam. I always had a pelvic ultrasound, transvaginal sonography, and the CA125 test which measured the level in my blood of a certain serum tumor marker. These were the best outpatient screening devices available. They were certainly advanced since my mother's day, as were the techniques of radiation and chemotherapy if I did get ovarian cancer. But early detection, the only real defense against the disease, was an impossibility. Of the tens of thousands of women diagnosed with ovarian cancer each year, over half died. The ovaries are hidden deep inside the pelvis, and the lack of external evidence—a lump in the breast that can be felt, a skin lesion that can be seen—blocks early detection. Even when ovarian cancer is as advanced as it was in my mother's case, the symptoms are often vague enough to be interpreted as indigestion or middle-aged weight gain. My mother's death had been terrible, it had been the shipwreck of my early life, but it was a common story for ovarian cancer: seventy-five percent of women

Laura Furman and her son

are diagnosed when the ovarian cancer has spread outside the ovaries and into the peritoneum. I would always be waiting.

On the other hand, my doctor told me, the surgery was major surgery, carrying with it the risks of general anesthesia, and afterward I would be on hormone replacement therapy, which had risks and benefits also. Taking estrogen meant a possible, if still unproved, risk of breast cancer. If I didn't take estrogen, my chances of osteoporosis and, possibly, heart disease increased.

My doctor gave me some material to read including the newsletter of the Gilda Radner Ovarian Cancer Registry, Roswell Park Cancer Institute, and relevant sections from an up-to-date gynecological textbook. When I learned that there was such a thing as familial ovarian cancer syndrome, I tried to find a way of predicting what my chances were.

The newsletter covered two sides of a single sheet of paper. I read it many times, trying to understand the unfamiliar vocabulary and to see where I fit into their recommendations. There was so much I didn't know then: my maternal grandmother's cause of death and all the other female relatives I had never heard about, whose names I'd never know, all the way back to the inaccessible *shtetls*.

First-degree relatives are those who share genes that are fifty-percent identical: mother, sister, daughter. Grandmothers and aunts are second degree. With two or more first-degree relatives with ovarian cancer, women have an even risk, fifty-fifty. With one first-degree and one second-degree, the chance is somewhat less than fifty percent. For women at high risk, the Registry newsletter recommended genetic counseling and a biannual examination including ultrasound and the CA125 test, followed by prophylactic oophorectomy (surgical removal of the ovaries and uterus) after the age of thirty-five or whenever childbearing was finished. I called the Registry and was told that with one first-degree relative, surgery wasn't necessarily recommended. It would have been a great reassurance if it had been.

I was tempted to bow my head and to give up, to live with the risk of ovarian cancer in a world full of risks, but I continued to wonder involuntarily, during idle moments, how to prepare my son for my death, and, noticing this, I was unwilling to give up the idea of being free of the disease.

One night when Solomon was asleep, I showed Joel the newsletter and the other material I had read on ovarian cancer. We were sitting at the granite table in the kitchen, a high table, cool to the touch, resting on a black-painted iron frame. He read the newsletter carefully, referring from one side to the other as I watched. We had talked before about the possibility of surgery. He had dreaded the prospect of the surgery but when he was finished reading the newsletter, he looked up and said that he thought the risks seemed too great to ignore. Whether my chances were fifty-fifty or thirty-seventy didn't matter to him. We had a great deal to lose and nothing to gain from a gamble.

My decision would have been easier if there had been a gene test to take or if I had fit the Registry's standards and been able to say, Yes, first-degree and second-degree, but I couldn't. Reassurance came after action in my case.

I had to be willing to trust an idea of healing as sufficient motive for the surgery. It seemed a version of my mother's surgery, the one I had blamed for her death, since at first I had thought that it was her visit to the hospital that had made her ill. I had to be rational and I had to find a way to be at peace in order to undergo the surgery with a good spirit.

I felt as though nothing I had done before would be so life-changing, though I had left New York to live in the country, left Fly Summit to move to Texas, married and adopted our son. If I survived the normal risks of surgery, then I would live a different life each subsequent day. I wouldn't be sad when I looked at my son, imagining that I wouldn't see him into adulthood. I would be able to think about many other things, once I'd rid myself of my constant anxiety about the death my body held. The operation, in fact, would restore my body to me as it had been before my mother's death, certainly not in its youth but in its health. I could trust my body when it was no longer my mortal enemy.

When I spoke with my gynecologist again, he was in agreement with me. His personal method of evaluation when a patient was facing a tough choice was to ask what he would want his wife to do were she in the patient's position. In my case, he would want her to have the surgery. He had stayed neutral and waited until I'd made up my own mind before telling me what his personal advice would be.

For the first time since my mother's death, I might be free of the possibility that I would die of ovarian cancer. I could decide, and did, to take my chances with the risks of anesthesia and estrogen therapy. I could live with those risks. A fear still abiding was that the surgery would reveal that ovarian cancer was already present. When I felt that particular fear rising, I breathed in deeply and let out air, saying, *So be it.*

I had needed faith to marry and faith to adopt my son and become a mother. Now I needed to have faith not only in my ability to make the right decision, but also in the outcome of the operation. I needed the faith a person has, not necessarily in God, but in the goodness of life and in things working out more or less well, most of the time. It was a humble faith I needed, the kind I had once had and lost at my mother's death. Now, my eyes on my own child, I struggled to regain it.

❧

Joel's parents said they'd come up and stay with Solomon while

I was in the hospital, so I knew that he and Joel would be all right.

The most important person to provide for was Solomon. I would be gone for three days and after that I'd be unable for a long while to pick him up. I wouldn't be able to drive for weeks. I needed to let him know that I was going to go into a hospital and that I'd be home in a few days. I'd been away before and had always drawn calendars for him of the days I'd be gone and what he and Joel would do while I was away. I could do that again. I was having an operation, I told him, which was hard since he was so young and had only a small understanding of what a hospital was or surgery. I drove him past the hospital a few times. It wasn't a comforting-looking building, but at least he knew where I would be. I went to our favorite children's bookstore and tried to find a story book to help me explain, but all I could find was *Curious George Goes to the Hospital* and *Going to the Hospital* by Mr. Rogers, both books meant to soothe children who have to be patients. I wondered if he would worry that he was going to the hospital and not I. He wasn't too interested in either book.

I gave thought to writing Solomon a letter in case I did die in surgery, and I composed it at odd times as I made the drive from Lockhart to Austin, always when I was alone in the car. In the end, I never wrote it.

∾

No one came right out and said that I was crazy. The intake nurse when I went to the hospital for blood work a few days before surgery asked if I really had to have the surgery and who was my doctor? When I told her, she looked puzzled. He was such a good doctor, such a good reputation. A friend whose mother had died of ovarian cancer asked me if I really wanted to lose my ovaries. Another friend asked if my doctor thought it was such a good idea, as if I might have sweet-talked him into it. I discovered, in short, that many people I knew were terrified of surgery in general and that many women were attached to their ovaries, perhaps as the symbol and source of their femininity. With a history of infertility, infections, and the possibility of ovarian cancer, I was a lot less attached to my ovaries than they were to theirs. My closest friends were supportive, even relieved for me, and I joked with them that a side benefit would be that I'd never have my period again. When I was alone that seemed a loss, a sign that I was changing myself irreversibly.

I told neither my sisters nor my stepmother until the operation was a fait accompli. I wrote them letters which I mailed on the way to the hospital. I knew that none of them had power over me, but I felt about them as a friend said she felt about her difficult marriage: "It's like in winter, when you take off your hat and all the heat escapes from your body." I needed all my heat for myself.

∾

The morning of the surgery, Joel and I drove Solomon to day care and then we went to the hospital. In the room I toured the pocket-sized bathroom with handles everywhere, wondering if I'd need them to stand and sit. I hung my clothes in the closet and put on a hospital gown and got into bed. Joel settled into the slippery armchair with a mystery. I tried to read, glancing up at the wall at every paragraph and forgetting the names of the characters. My doctor appeared in surgical blues to tell me that my operation had to be delayed but for no more than an hour and a half. A woman in late pregnancy was having some trouble. I thought it might be a sign that I should get out, but it had taken me such a long time to get to that room, and a few hours didn't seem too long to wait.

∾

Joel was with me in the room when I woke up. The dressing felt like a little pillow on my abdomen. The doctor came in later, woke me up and told me my ovaries and uterus had looked just fine to him and that he'd sent them on to the lab for biopsy. The next time I woke, Joel had gone to pick up Solomon and take him home to Lockhart before returning to stay the night with me. My friend Susan sat in the visitor's chair, reading a book. She smiled a beatific smile at me and told me that she'd heard her baby's heartbeat just a few hours before. I waited for the envy that I'd always felt at news of a friend's pregnancy and instead felt happiness for my friend and her baby, a new person I would someday get to know.

There were flowers all over the room, on every possible surface. When I felt pain the first afternoon and night, there was my Demerol pump. The next day I was up and walking, not far and not fast but I was walking. The hospital floor was almost empty that weekend, so even when I made it all the way to the nursery there were no babies to see. The few newborns were with their mothers in their rooms. The Demerol pump was replaced by pills. The nurses urged me not to rush back to work. When I went home, they told me to make my bed while I was in it to spare myself stretching. I was being welcomed into a sisterhood I hadn't known existed. I left the hospital at mid-day the third day after surgery.

∾

I was never in terrible pain during the six-week recovery but it was hard to summon the energy to do much of anything. I had imagined that at last I would read all of *Remembrance of Things Past* but I didn't. I forced myself up from bed to make dinner as soon as I could walk but it was frozen dinners at best. My older sister sent flowers. My stepmother called to say that I'd done the right thing. My bed was covered with books, and books were stacked on the floor next to me because I was on a panel judging writers for a prize. I completed deadline work on a journal I was editing. Everything was different but it was all the same. I spoke on the phone with friends until my ear hurt. One of my oldest friends called from Kentucky to say that if there were a way for him to have something removed to stop him meeting his father's fate, he would do it, but his father, we recalled, had died of a brain tumor.

The pathologist's report came in: all clear.

In order to press my insurance company into paying for a surgery they felt was medically unnecessary (a fight I won eventually), I had to pursue the family history I had lost along with my mother. I called my sister Valerie and asked if she knew where to find our cousins, and the next day I spoke to Molly's daughter. Aunt Molly had died years before but I wasn't sure of the exact cause, and I thought my cousin might know what our Aunt Sophie had died of also.

My cousin was still in New York. She was a schoolteacher, spoke daily to her younger sister who lived in California, and to her father who had remarried after Molly's death. I described the surgery I'd just undergone ("What a way to cut the cord!" she said), and asked her my questions. Neither Molly nor Sophie had developed ovarian cancer, she said, but Grandma Ida had died of it. She was surprised I didn't know that and, though she was younger than I and our grandmother had died before either of us had been born, she spoke of her as if she'd known her. I had never before heard Ida's name.

My cousin suggested that I call her father, and his recollection was that Ida had died in August 1944 in Atlanta of ovarian cancer. When I got the death certificate weeks later from the Georgia Department of Public Health, I saw she'd died around my mother's birthday: Carcinoma of the Ovary. I imagined the long train trip south my mother had made to the funeral with my sister Valerie, who had just had her second birthday.

My grandmother's death from ovarian cancer changed my odds and put me in the slightly less than fifty-fifty category, with one first-degree and one second-degree relative. I called the Ovarian Cancer Registry in Buffalo again, this time to register my family in their long-term study. In doing so I felt that I was giving some care to the unrecognized dead, and some hope to the living.

∽

In the days and weeks after the surgery I felt waves of sadness, the feeling that someone or something was missing. A friend had given me a young-adult novel because I was thinking of writing one, perhaps for the young adult I had been. One afternoon I started crying as I read, and then my crying developed into wracking sobs. My mother was gone. I had betrayed her by having the surgery. I had differentiated myself from her and said, *I will not end as you did.* By rejecting the disease that had killed my mother, by being willing to part with the organs that had killed her, I was afraid I was losing her forever. I recalled once again the distortion of her body and the pain of her disease, and my crushing sense of being left by her.

As I healed, these overwhelming visual and emotional images of my mother gradually took their place in a more balanced sense of her life and mine. Slowly I regained her as she had been as my mother, strong and healthy, as she was during my development from infant to toddler to young child to early adolescent. Then—as if I had been given permission—I remembered my adolescence and youth. I hadn't lost those years. I didn't have such a terrible memory after all, only one which had dwelled for a long time in one place.

I could live to be ninety, my doctor said when he examined me six weeks after surgery. It has taken me a while to understand what that possibility means. I am living a second life, and I live it differently, more slowly and hopefully, with less desire to hurry my experiences along against my mother's premature end.

∿

About a year after the surgery, we moved from Lockhart to Austin. I threw away many things that were broken and had other things repaired—rugs, picture frames, furniture. Remembering my father's bedside table, I discarded old tax forms and letters, gave away clothing and records, books, dishes, anything that didn't any longer suit me or my life as I lived it in the present. Since I'd never done such a thorough cleaning and ordering, I was clearing away things I'd carried from West End Avenue to Fly Summit and across Texas.

My first winter in our new house, I woke before dawn most mornings and met a friend at Barton Springs, a pool an eighth of a mile long, set in the middle of the city's central park, and filled with spring water that is sixty-eight degrees all year round, part of Barton Creek as it flows through Austin. The pool is long enough to lose yourself dreaming as you swim each length. Often in the winter the water was warmer than the air, causing mist, and as I turned my head to breathe I saw ducks gliding past me and heard them calling to one another. When I lowered my head into the water, I saw fish moving below and, once, startlingly, I bumped into a fish in the dark. Three times each morning I swam to the line of light where sunrise was beginning and back into darkness and the paler light of the moon. Then my friend and I dried off and went to sit on a bench above the Springs and drink coffee.

There were other swimmers there, more as the light came,

and I took a particular interest in the very old people who managed with varying degrees of difficulty to make it down the many steps to the water, disrobe, set aside their canes or braces, and sink into the water where they were free of their incapacities. Some swam, some treaded in a circle of swimmers who met there each morning. I watched the water with my friend, and we talked about being those old people in two or three or four more decades. I was amazed to be thinking such things, to be there at all.